HERE'S WHAT OTHERS ARE SAYING ABOUT RAISING MORE MONEY...

After only four months of Point of Entry Events we had 120 people at our first free ask luncheon, and we raised over $138,000. We know that implementing this model over the next few years will take our fundraising efforts to the next level. Terry, thank you.
> — David Foubert, Vice President, Development
> Otterbein Retirement Living Communities, Lebanon, OH

The Raising More Money Model confirmed what we have practiced intuitively for years—that deepening relationships will lead to lifelong donors. We are thankful to Raising More Money for giving us a system that takes the mystery and fear out of fundraising.
> — Mark A. Finser, President
> Rudolf Steiner Foundation, San Francisco, CA

Our Point of Entry Events are a huge success! Through them, we have increased our season ticket sales, recruited volunteers, gained board members, and raised what for us is a good deal of money.
> — Kathryn Fellows, Executive Director
> Mesa Symphony Orchestra, AZ

Thanks to the Raising More Money process, development professionals around the world are thinking and acting differently. I am grateful for the opportunity to develop lifelong donors based on the concepts and training I received from Raising More Money.
> — Finley Green, President
> Junior Achievement Tri-Cities TN/VA

We knew there was a better way—we found it with Raising More Money. Raising More Money enabled us to concentrate on what is most important—building lifelong relationships with those who care about our mission—while at the same time helping us raise significant, multi-year, unrestricted gifts.
> — Rev. Elliot Smith, Vice President for Development
> Presbyterian Children's Homes and Services, Austin, TX

Using the Raising More Money approach, we have implemented a systematic way of establishing and enriching relationships with individuals in our community. Among these individuals are our newly found lifelong believers—those that spread our word, volunteer for us, and support us financially, year after year.
 — **Mark Russell, Executive Director**
   The Arc of Northern Virginia

The Raising More Money workshop provided our young organization with a fundraising model that is concrete, simple and comprehensive. This system-driven approach can be implemented immediately, and it utilizes our greatest strength—our mission!
 — **Gary Landwirth, President**
   A Gift for Teaching, Orlando, FL

Raising More Money demystifies the whole scary process of individual fundraising—but the most important thing it gave me was the courage and confidence to ask people to support our mission.
 — **Mary Donnelly-Crocker, Executive Director**
   Young & Healthy, Pasadena, CA

I have been a professional fundraiser for 13 years. Raising More Money brings together all the common-sense fundraising approaches in one tried-and-true model. Mission-driven and permission-based fundraising truly creates a partnership between the organization and donor. This is the basis of the Raising More Money Model, which is why it works!
 — **Sharon Bosserman-Benson, Director of Advancement**
   Community Action Organization, Hillsboro, OR

Raising More Money has provided us the tools for leaving the legacy of a consistent, reliable system that can continue to sustain our charity.
 — **John Rynne, General Manager**
   Ronald McDonald House Charities, Queensland, Australia

RAISING MORE M NEY

THE
POINT OF ENTRY
HANDBOOK

TERRY AXELROD

Raising More Money
The Point of Entry Handbook
Terry Axelrod

Raising More Money Publications, Seattle, Washington
The following trademarks appear throughout this book:
Raising More Money Model™, the Raising More Money Workshop™
and Raising More Money E-New$™.

ISBN: 0-9700455-2-2

Library of Congress Control Number: 2002104548

ATTENTION CORPORATIONS, UNIVERSITIES,
COLLEGES, AND PROFESSIONAL ORGANIZATIONS:
Quantity discounts are available on bulk purchases
of this book for educational purposes.
Special books or book excerpts can also be created to fit specific needs.
For information, please contact:
Raising More Money Publications
1301 Spring Street, Suite 7E
Seattle, WA 98104
Phone 888-322-9357

BENEFITS OF THE RAISING MORE MONEY APPROACH

- Gives your organization a system for tapping into the 85% of all contributions that come from individuals

- Focuses on fundraising as a science, rather than an art

- Continuously builds your base of lifelong donors; gets you off the treadmill

- Allows your organization to establish a multiple-year unrestricted giving society

- Mission-based; honors your donors' true commitment to your work

- Includes everything you are already doing right

- Treats donors the way you would want to be treated:

  - Permission-based; no more strong-arming

  - Organic; allows time for donors to become educated, inspired and involved before being asked for money

Also by Terry Axelrod:

Raising More Money:
A Step-by-Step Guide to Building Lifelong Donors

ACKNOWLEDGMENTS

The sole reason this book was written was because of the number of requests from subscribers to our free electronic newsletter —Raising More Money E-New$—and from participants in our workshops, for more detailed information about Points of Entry.

If anyone had told me seven years ago, when we held the first Raising More Money workshop, that there would be a "demand" for a Point of Entry Handbook, I would have laughed. Therefore, my sincere thanks go first to our loyal subscribers and participants who have adopted the model—in whole or in part—and have continued to dig for more specific information. It tells me just how serious you are about this and about fulfilling the missions of your organizations.

Next, I would like to acknowledge our exceptional staff, including our instructors and coaches, who either arrived with or quickly inherited the passion for Raising More Money. Their unwavering commitment to serving each and every one of the nonprofit organizations we have the privilege of working with staggers me. We attempt to follow the Raising More Money Model in the day-to-day operation of our organization, so this is about a lot more to them than a book.

I'd like to again acknowledge Seth Godin, author of *Permission Marketing*, for talking so straight about building relationships and for blowing the lid off the old heavy-handed "sales" approach once and for all. His work continues to inspire me.

As a neophyte author, I continue to be amazed at what it takes to write and publish a book. For the steadfast advice and hand of my editor Ann Overton, I am so grateful. Her incisive input guided and blessed every step of the way. Special thanks and congratulations to in-house editor Dina Trageser for her diligent work in taking this full cycle, and in such good humor—a trait I envy.

And finally, to my husband and partner in all things, Alan Axelrod, for coming to my defense the first night of the now familiar dinner-table refrain from our two teenagers: What's a Point of Entry anyway, Mom, and how much more can you really say about it? Thanks for always making it so much fun.

TABLE OF CONTENTS

PREFACE

Since its inception in 1996, Raising More Money has become a successful model for generating self-sustaining funding from individual donors for nonprofit organizations of all types and sizes. Whether your work focuses on health and human services, environmental protection, the arts, public policy, faith-based programs, social justice or other issues, the Raising More Money Model can be customized to your organization and implemented successfully.

This Point of Entry Handbook is written for people both new to and familiar with Raising More Money. Knowing that for some of you this may be your first exposure to Raising More Money, I have included a brief overview of the entire model to set the Point of Entry in context. This overview is not intended to be a substitute for the first book, *Raising More Money—A Step-by-Step Guide to Building Lifelong Donors*, which goes into more depth on many other components of the model, not addressed here.

Why write a handbook for Points of Entry? What is a Point of Entry anyway, and why is it so important that it warrants a book of its own—a handbook, a rule book, a book that purports to be the definitive source on Points of Entry?

This book is in response to the remarkable number of questions we receive on our Web site and in person from people who have read *Raising More Money—A Step-by-Step Guide to Building Lifelong Donors*. Having begun to implement the four-step model, they get a sense of the power of the Point of Entry and become much more serious about how to "do it right."

The Point of Entry is the cornerstone of the Raising More

Money Model, the mission-based system for building lifelong donors. In addition to being the quintessential introductory event about
your nonprofit organization, its program elements are essential to
each of the other three steps in the model. People are invited word-
of-mouth by someone they trust to attend a one-hour introductory
event about your organization. They know in advance that you are
looking to spread the word and gather feedback about the programs
and services provided. They know in advance that they will not be
asked to give money at a Point of Entry. It is a safe, permission-based
way for new people to kick the tires and see if there is any way they
might want to become involved.

The person who greets them at the Point of Entry becomes the
one who shepherds the guests through the process for the next year
and longer, should they choose to become involved. This is the person who follows up with them after their first Point of Entry Event
to get their feedback and see if they are even interested in continuing
their relationship with the organization. There is absolutely no obligation for any guest to go further.

Without a free-to-choose introductory event like a Point of
Entry, people will presume your organization operates the "old way."
They will assume there is some unspoken obligation to give money
at the end of the tour or introductory session. At that point they
would most likely be giving to allay a sense of guilt and obligation to
their friend who invited them to attend. They will feel manipulated
and pressured and confused as to exactly what is being asked of them,
yet they will never tell you that. Instead, they will make a one-time
gift and move on.

Although taking people through the Point of Entry process may
delay the actual first gift by six to nine months, by that time the
guests will have been sufficiently introduced, inspired and involved
to whatever extent they choose. Therefore, their first gift will be a
real contribution, rather than a one-time gift to placate a friend. You
will have planted the seeds for a lifelong relationship with a donor
who is giving freely to the mission and fine work of your organization. As such, when the donor's friend goes off your board, the donor
will continue to give for the right reasons.

This model honors the mission of each nonprofit organization. It honors the natural intent of our donors to make a difference with their money. It lets the fruit ripen at its own natural pace. It may not get you every dollar you had dreamed of from every major donor in the first year, but in the long run you will have served the organization and the donor by building a solid lifelong relationship. Whether these donors become key board members or Table Captains at your annual Free One-Hour Ask Event, they will be doing it for the right reasons.

The integrity of the model has got to be palpable in the guest's first exposure to your organization. For them, it all begins with the Point of Entry. To be true to the Raising More Money Model, it's got to be done "by the book," so to speak. Here is the book.

RAISING MORE MONEY:
THE BIG PICTURE

CHAPTER 1

MISSION-BASED FUNDRAISING

People often refer to the Raising More Money Model as "mission-based" fundraising. They find it to be a huge relief that they can actually talk straight to people about their work without having to sugarcoat what they are doing. They find it enormously refreshing to know that, once they have adopted this approach, they are on a perpetual scouting expedition to find individuals who are naturally passionate about and interested in their mission. They seem to be surprised at first to discover that those very same people they walk by at the coffee shop or sit next to on the bus, or the other parents at their children's schools might actually *care*—in their own right—about the work of their organizations.

Armed with that insight, they become freed up to be the natural walking ambassadors they are for their missions. Suddenly they have license to let their natural passion out. "Oh," they say. "Is that all you want us to do? To tell other people about our work and why we think it's so important? Are you telling us that is what's needed in fundraising?"

They see that they have all it takes. They don't need to know how to put on a special event, they don't need to take up golf, or join a fancy club where they can rub shoulders with rich people. In fact, they begin to see that the lifelong donors their organizations deserve might be lurking right there under their noses—or in their databases. Perhaps those mission-based, potential lifelong donors are the very people who already give small amounts to them faithfully each

3

month or year through the mail. Or perhaps they are people who hardly know the organization exists; yet they have a family member who has benefited indirectly from its services. Perhaps they are lying undiscovered among the organization's vendors, volunteers or former volunteers, or its former grateful hospital patients or alumni.

Think for a moment about the notion of a lifelong donor. Odds are you are already on your way to becoming a lifelong donor for at least one of your favorite organizations. They may not do much to keep in touch with you. In fact, they may not even know you personally at all. Yet you feel connected enough to their work that you can pretty much already predict you will give them money for many years to come.

Why is that? What did they do to deserve your loyalty and support? Perhaps a member of your family has the disease they seek to cure. Perhaps you met someone once whose life you will always want to honor with a gift to a particular organization. Or perhaps, as one wonderful river protection organization once told me, "Everyone has a river they have known and loved in their life." Maybe it is because that particular river or organization just happened to be there and touch your life.

In our incredibly fast-changing world, people are hungry for meaningful connections. What once seemed like a token check arriving in the mail may be much more. That simple act, that simple gift, may represent a lifetime of hope for someone. Whether the check is for $10, $1000 or $1,000,000, people are telling you something with those gifts. They are placing their vote with your organization. They are saying they believe that your work is making a difference. They understand enough about what you are doing to vote for you to keep doing more and better work.

We tell people in our workshops that it takes two things to be good at raising money from individuals: a deep and abiding passion for the organization's mission, and a system. You have to have a system.

Every nonprofit organization has systems in place for delivering their programs and services. The Red Cross has a particular way of teaching us CPR. They don't leave it up to the whim of the instructor each day to come up with a new system. Likewise, Habitat for

Humanity has a brilliant system for getting houses built. I once saw a list of the supplies they needed for a forty-house "blitz-build." It was detailed enough to include the number of pounds of nails, number of hammers and the number of lunches. It even included the number of massage tables! They have a system.

Yet when it comes to raising funds, most nonprofits are still in trial-and-error mode. The basic diet consists of grant writing, a few special events and some direct-mail solicitations. This leaves them on the treadmill of year-to-year, hand-to-mouth begging, entertaining, strong-arming and manipulating relative strangers to make gifts out of guilt and obligation—gifts they may later resent. It does not propagate lifelong donors. It propagates the need to constantly find new one-time donors, and it builds nothing for the organization's future. As donors, this approach dishonors our natural interest and commitment to the mission of certain organizations. Furthermore, it dishonors and degrades the vital work each organization is doing by presuming it is not worthy of people's long-term support.

The fundraising paradigm has shifted. As the futurists tell us, when a paradigm shifts, everything goes back to zero. Any mastery and expertise you had in the old paradigm counts for nothing. Everyone is starting over together. They say it takes about ten to fifteen years before people realize they are living in a new paradigm—and by then the paradigm has shifted again.

We are probably one or two paradigms beyond the days of begging and sacrificial giving. Just as we have adapted day by day to the incredible infusion of new technology in our personal lives, so has the world of giving changed around us incrementally.

Any effective fundraising system must operate consistently with the prevailing paradigm. Therefore, before we delve into the nuts and bolts of the Points of Entry, we need to back up and look at the defining characteristics of the new paradigm, or the new fundraising reality.

DEFINING CHARACTERISTICS OF THE NEW FUNDRAISING REALITY

Resources Are Abundant

In the old reality, there was never enough. We never had to stop and ask ourselves whether or not there was enough of anything; we just knew there wasn't. If you worked in the nonprofit world, and especially if you worked in the development field, your job was to carry the torch, to dutifully carry the heavy load. You accepted the challenge of accomplishing the important work of your organization in the face of inadequate resources. Scarcity was a given.

In the new reality, resources are abundant. Over $200 billion was given to charitable organizations in the United States in the year 2000, eighty-three percent of which was contributed by individuals. The Newtithing Institute, a philanthropic research organization based in San Francisco, found that in the year 2001 alone, individual giving in the United States could easily have been increased by $127 billion without significantly affecting anyone's lifestyle.

This is key in shaping the future of nonprofit organizations. The organizations that recognize that the new reality is paved with abundant resources and generous people wanting to contribute will be the organizations that will thrive.

Leaving the Legacy of a System

In the old reality of scarcity, you were thankful for whatever you could get. This ensured the perpetuation of the hunter-gatherer approach to fundraising. "Quick: we need money. Let's do whatever we have to do to get it right now." There was not much looking out towards the horizon. We were locked into that year-to-year, stay-on-the-treadmill approach. Unless you were fortunate enough to work with one of the blue-chip established charitable organizations, you were destined to wage near hand-to-hand combat, fighting for your existence one year at a time.

Successful fundraising in the new reality requires a commitment to leaving a legacy, not merely doing a job for a few years. It requires leadership in stating what that legacy will be and then making it happen.

Imagine if you could leave your organization with the legacy of a system—a step-by-step recipe for building lifelong donors. It would be customized for the way your organization operates with your donors. It would have built-in reminders, not dependent on one well-organized staff person, to tell you, for example, when three months have passed since anyone has talked to those first-time donors. It would tell you how each donor preferred to be contacted: by phone, by mail or online.

What if you could leave that legacy for the next generation at your organization? Instead of inheriting the predictable hand-to-mouth, year-to-year existence, the person who replaces you could inherit a database filled with people who are well known to your organization, people who have been giving for many years because they so believe in your mission.

The short-term thinking of the old reality made it nearly impossible to do any future long-term fiscal planning, let alone dream of building an endowment. In fact, once you can let go of the old-reality attachment to scarcity and recognize the importance of having a self-sustaining individual giving system, you will be able to look out over the horizon to the future.

If your organization is at least ten years old, you should actively be implementing a plan to build an endowment that throws off enough interest to cover your operating shortfall each year. While that sum of money may seem enormous to you, until you quantify it and clarify how you would invest the funds and spend the earnings, the old reality may be getting in the way of donors who are right there with you, wanting to give.

Today's donors don't want to hear your sad story. They want to hear your plan. Tell them the facts; share your passion, your fears about where you might be losing ground. They can take it.

What would it mean to you to be able to leave the legacy of a system to fund unrestricted operating needs forever?

Individual Donors Are the Key

In the old reality, many nonprofit organizations could get by just fine without having to raise money from individuals. The predominant sources of "private" funding were grants from corporations and foundations or funding from United Way. Any funds raised from individuals were considered to be the icing on the cake.

In the new reality, individual donors will be the centerpiece of your fundraising strategy. Most organizations without a strong base of individual support will falter or fade away. Those organizations with a system for building and cultivating lifelong donors—donors who understand and feel connected to the work of the organization—will thrive.

There are four key points to note about individuals as donors:

1. We all give. In the United States, nearly 90% of the population gives money to charitable causes.

2. As individuals, we are loyal donors. Most of us have been giving year after year to a core group of what I refer to as our "default charities." In good times and in bad times, these organizations make it to the top of our giving list. These are the organizations we care about and feel connected to.

3. As individuals, statistically, our disposable income increases as we get older. At least in theory, we have more to give away.

4. Unlike corporations or foundations, in the end individuals have to give it all away. Corporations and foundations only give away the interest. Individuals give away the principal.

Focus on Deepening Relationships with Existing Donors

Because the old reality was based in scarcity and survival, and because the majority of our fundraising efforts were focused on corporations and foundations, cultivating longer-term relationships with donors seemed much too time-consuming. It was easier and quicker to get more new donors each year. Given the baby-boomer bulge in population, this strategy seemed to work. There seemed to be an unending supply of new donors. It was quick and impersonal.

But as any smart marketing person will tell you, it costs at least five times as much to acquire a new donor as to renew and upgrade an existing donor.

In the new reality, instead of spending time acquiring more donors, you could spend time deepening your relationship with the ones you already have. You might be surprised to learn how many of them would love to become lifelong donors.

A True Dialog with Your Donors

In the old reality, we were perfectly satisfied with having a monolog with our donors. We would blurt out our needs and the ideal response was for the donor to send money. We often did not feel the need to talk to them directly or engage them in an ongoing conversation.

In the new reality, donors want to be more connected to you. This does not mean they necessarily want to give you more time. It means that they want to be more connected than merely receiving your quarterly newsletter in the mail. They want to know that you are interested in them; that they are special to you. What must they do in order to get your attention? Without that, they will go next door or down the street to a charitable organization that will appreciate their interest.

As soon as you begin to engage your donors in meaningful dialog, you have stepped into the new reality. This type of dialog is no longer optional. It is essential for keeping your organization fresh and vital in the new reality. You have to want to know what your donors think.

Appreciating the Donor Next Door

In the old reality, the ideal donor had been clearly identified. He was an older, white, wealthy male. We knew just where to find him and just who should ask him. We can say goodbye to that reality.

In the new reality, *everyone* is a potential donor and, quite possibly, a potential major donor. In fact, part of the new American dream is to become a philanthropist. People actually *aspire* to give money away.

Let's look at the statistics:

There is at least one person in at least seventy percent of U.S. households who donates money to a charitable organization. That means that at least three out of four households give. Furthermore, the demographics of individual donors mirror the ethnic, age and gender diversity of today's communities. If you want to know who your future donors will be, just track these trends in your community.

For example, we are already seeing far greater age diversity in our donors. Many people are capable of making more substantial gifts at younger ages. In addition, the majority of donors are women. If you were designing your program to be consistent with these trends, you would seek out and develop lifelong relationships with women donors in their own right, treating each woman as a potential major donor beginning with the Point of Entry.

The New Volunteer/Donor

A recent study shows that of all the adults who volunteered in 2001, ninety-five percent also gave to charitable causes. Also, the households in which a respondent volunteered gave over twice as much as the non-volunteer households.

This gives the term "volunteer" a whole new meaning. The edges of "volunteer" blur with the edges of "donor." Those organizations that treat volunteers as lifelong major donors will thrive. Conversely, they will treat donors as volunteers or potential volunteers.

In the new reality, volunteer programs will be operated hand-in-hand with fundraising programs.

Asking Naturally

In the old reality, the shorthand description of asking for money could be called "strong-arming the Rolodex." In the new reality, by the time you get around to asking someone for money, it should be nothing more than nudging the inevitable. Unless you know the person is ready to give, you shouldn't ask them. Asking for a contribution would be no more stressful than picking the low-hanging fruit off a tree.

Cultivating donor relationships requires what is now called "permission marketing" in the business world. The term, coined by high-tech marketing guru Seth Godin, says that we must earn people's permission to market to them, each step of the way. If you take the time to do that, donors will feel as if they are part of your organization's family. If you honor that they truly believe in and support your mission, they will stay with you forever.

Multiple-Year Unrestricted Pledges

Once you begin to regard your donors as your partners in fulfilling your mission, you will naturally see that many of them would be delighted to promise to give to you for many years in the future. After all, in their minds, they have already decided to do so.

Once you know them well, it would be almost insulting if you did not invite them to be a part of your organization's family by making a pledge to your Multiple-Year Giving Society. While it is true that their pledge is not a guarantee of a future gift, it provides a powerful vehicle for these special donors to demonstrate their longer-term commitment.

For many donors in your Multiple-Year Giving Society, this unrestricted gift is just a starter gift. They may actually be interested in and capable of giving you more. Their pledge is telling you that they are real believers. They are giving you permission to come back and talk with them about other concerns and needs you may have.

Building Relationships Online

In the old reality, there were three ways people could give: by mail, by phone or in person.

Mail was easy for the organization: it could be contracted out and was relatively impersonal. No one on the staff had to interact with those scary real donors. There was plenty of demographic data available to tell us what they would want. We could presume that you and your neighbor who each drove the same type of car and lived in the same zip code were pretty much identical in your preferences. In other words, we didn't have to personalize our communication to you.

The second choice was phone. By using staff or volunteer callers or by contracting with professional telemarketing firms, we did not have to get to know our donors.

Asking in person clearly yielded the greatest results. It gave us contact with the immediate decision makers. Yet it meant having to make all those "I-hate-fundraising" people do something they really didn't want to do.

In the new reality, each of these forms of contact also becomes a medium for building relationships and staying related to your donors. However, if you look at how we relate day-to-day, you will notice one medium is missing from our list: e-mail.

Rather than thinking of the Internet as a place for one-time donors to click and give, consider the power of e-mail to establish and build relationships over time. Also, do not overlook the Internet as a simpler giving vehicle for those donors who are already relating to you in person.

While nothing will ever replace the quality of a face-to-face relationship, online relating, by its very nature, offers precisely the customized, personalized dialog so essential in the new reality. It will become the preferred medium of many of your donors for relating to your organization.

IMPLEMENTING THE SYSTEM: WHY BOTHER?

The Raising More Money system is designed to operate consistently with these principles of the new fundraising paradigm. That is why so many organizations have so much success with this approach. It provides a system that educates and inspires donors, involves them however they would like to become involved, and asks them to give unrestricted gifts of increasing sizes for many years to come. They do all this for the right reasons: because they truly understand and believe in what you're up to.

If you are to be successful with the Raising More Money Model, you will need to decide for yourself why it would be worth it to you to go to the work of implementing this model in your organization.

After all, when you introduce anything new within an organization, there is bound to be resistance. People have become accustomed to the old familiar way, even if they know it was not particularly effective. If you are to be the champion of this new, mission-based approach, odds are you are going to encounter resistance. Are you prepared for that?

Before you embark on this bold new endeavor, ask yourself: "What is the legacy I am committed to leaving for this organization? What is the one thing I most want to see happen here before I leave? What is the one thing that would make me happiest to accomplish, even if no one else ever recognizes my role in having brought it about?"

Would you want to have left the legacy of better salaries for the staff, a well-funded scholarship program, services made available to more people, an endowment fund? What is the thing that you are most passionate about seeing through? Would that be a legacy worth leaving?

Without having thought through your answer to this question, it would be easy to back down when the first obstacle appears, rather than recognizing it as a natural part of the path. You will need to be crystal-clear about why you're doing this; any hesitancy or tentativeness on your part will be easily detected by others. Conversely, your clear vision of what you are out to accomplish will naturally attract people.

To help you determine what legacy you would like to leave for your organization, consider doing this quick exercise that we use in the Raising More Money Workshop: Imagine for a moment that you were to leave your organization and not come back for twenty years. When you do come back, no one recognizes you, of course. As you snoop around, you notice that things seem to be going very well. That mission statement that you had posted on the wall back in your day seems to be getting fulfilled—better health care for the children, more services to the elderly, higher literacy rates, more environmental protection, whatever it was. In fact, they are doing just great without you. As you snoop around a bit more, realize that there is one thing distinctly different from the years when you were there: no one seems to be worrying any more about the money. In fact, it seems as though they have plenty of money. All of their focus now is on fulfilling the mission.

Of course, you get up your courage to ask someone: "Excuse me, back in my day, it seemed as though we were always worrying about the money. What happened?"

"Oh, the money," they say. "We handled that ten or fifteen years ago. Now we can just focus on the work to be done."

Of course, you can't resist asking the next question: "What happened then—ten or fifteen years ago?"

I say the answer to that question is yours to fill in. What if you could be the person who could stem the tide on the old suffering, scarcity mentality and put an end to all that? What if you could leave the legacy of a self-sustaining system?

It would be a system that naturally generated more and more donors who truly believed in the mission of your organization. These donors would be giving because they wanted to give, not because they had been manipulated, strong-armed or entertained, but because they had chosen freely to make a contribution.

CHAPTER 2

THE RAISING MORE MONEY MODEL

The Raising More Money Model is a four-step system for building lifelong donors. It gives you a step-by-step recipe for success. And, just like any cherished family recipe, especially the first time you try it, you do not want to experiment with the formula. This is not the time for creativity; just follow the recipe.

Even if you are familiar with this approach, I recommend you read the description of the model again, to remind yourself of each step. This time, read with a focus on the essential role the Point of Entry plays in setting the tone of your relationship with your future donors and in telling your organization's story succinctly and powerfully.

IT'S A CIRCLE

The model is designed as a circle. Imagine a loop, a closed circuit, or an old-fashioned electric train set that just goes around and around. Once your potential donors get on board, they stay on board. The cycle starts over each time they give. Your job is to tailor this model to your organization and to keep expanding it to include as many people as possible, year after year.

The model has four essential steps, which take you through the cycle.

Step One: The Point of Entry

Potential donors get on the track at a Point of Entry. The Point of Entry is a one-hour introductory event that educates and inspires people about your organization. You do not ask for money at a Point of Entry. You should assume that every potential donor will attend only one Point of Entry Event in their lifetime, so it should be memorable.

STEP ONE: **THE POINT OF ENTRY**

A Point of Entry must include three components:

1. The basic information—the "Facts 101" about your organization, including the vision and needs;

2. An "Emotional Hook" so compelling people will never forget it; and

3. A system for "Capturing the Names," including addresses, phone numbers and e-mail addresses of the guests, with their permission.

Your Point of Entry must give people a sense of how the work of your organization changes lives. That is because, as individuals, we are emotional donors looking for rational reasons to justify our emotional decision to give. Your Point of Entry Event must satisfy both the head and the heart; neither the emotions nor the facts alone will do it. The Point of Entry must intertwine facts and emotion so that, before they even realize it, the guests are satisfied. If you don't accomplish both, you won't have a foundation from which to launch a relationship with a lifelong donor.

The **Facts 101** must include:

- A brief history of the organization;
- A basic statement of the programs and services offered;
- The numbers: people served, budget size, etc.; and
- The vision for the future, including a clear statement of what you will need to get there. You have to clearly identify the gap. You can easily do this while highlighting your strengths. "As wonderful as this program is, there are still 2,000 children in our area going unserved." "With just three more computers we could increase our efficiency immensely and spend more time serving people."

The **Emotional Hook** is most easily conveyed through stories, which may be presented in person by a staff member, family member or the actual person who benefited from your programs or services. Once you have identified the most representative story that is sure to capture people's emotions every time, you can tell this "Essential Story" and others like it using a variety of methods: a video or audio tape, a letter, a tour, or a dramatic or artistic presentation.

Finally, you must be sure you have a permission-based system to **Capture the Names**, addresses, phone numbers and e-mail addresses of every guest. After all, if the Point of Entry Event is just the first point in a cycle of lifelong giving, you will need to know how to contact each person again. Rather than tricking or manipulating them by pretending to collect their business cards for some other purpose, you will be able to ask people to fill out a card with their contact information, because they have been told in advance what to expect. They know they are coming to a brief introductory session to learn about a wonderful organization. They know that they will not be asked to give money at the Point of Entry. They are coming because they have been invited by a friend or other person who they trust.

Step Two: Follow Up and Involve

When people are invited to your organization's Point of Entry Events, they are told the truth: that you are trying to spread the word about your work and to solicit feedback about your programs from people in your community. After all, that is exactly what you are trying to do. However, the only way you will know what they really thought about your organization or your Point of Entry Event is if you ask them. If you are not planning on doing a rigorous job of following up with each and every person who attends a Point of Entry Event, there is no point in having Points of Entry at all. In fact, as we shall discuss in Chapter 13, the very first step in planning each event should be to design your follow-up system.

Therefore, the second step on the circle of a self-sustaining individual giving program is making a personal Follow-Up Call within a week to each person who attended the Point of Entry Event.

The Follow-Up Call is not a standard thank-you, for which a note would suffice. It is an interactive research call. Think of it as a one-on-one focus group in which you gather critical data on each potential lifelong donor and friend. The purpose of this call is to generate an authentic dialog with true give and take. If you think of the people with whom you have lifelong relationships—your friends and family—these relationships are rooted in a true dialog. It should be no different with your donors.

STEP TWO: **FOLLOW UP**

The Follow-Up Call follows a specific, five-point format that will help you get the information you need.

Point 1.

"Thank you for coming." You certainly need to thank them. They are busy people who did not need to take their time to come to your Point of Entry Event.

Point 2.

Ask: "What did you think (of the tour, the organization, the issue)?" Ask enough questions to get them talking.

Point 3.

Listen. This is the hardest step for most of us, and by far the most critical component of the Follow-Up Call. Stop talking and listen. In this model, the more you listen, the more you will notice that potential donors are telling you exactly how they would like to become involved with your organization. If you are too busy talking or planning what you want to say next, you will miss all the rich cues.

Point 4.

If they have not already told you, ask: "Is there any way you could see yourself becoming involved with our organization?" You let them tell you. In the new reality of donor-centered individual giving, the donors have their own ideas—ideas that may not mesh with your needs. You still need to listen and be open to saying yes to what they offer.

Point 5.

Finally, ask: "Is there anyone else you think we should invite to a Point of Entry Event?" You may be surprised to discover that, because you have taken the time to listen at each step along the way, people will be so appreciative they will naturally suggest others you should contact. Even people who are honest enough to tell you your issue is not their hot button will have other people for you to invite. Ask if they would mind if you contact these people directly and use their name. Then do it.

Every bit of data you gather should be recorded in your database. Be sure your computer system has a good section for you to record notes about each contact with each donor.

Letting People Off the Hook

You are sure to come across people who are not interested in getting more involved with your organization. The Follow-Up Call is where you can let them off the hook. Don't even think about taking it personally. Put yourself in their shoes. They took their time to come to the Point of Entry Event. Yes, they were touched and impressed with what you do, they may even send you a little check as a courtesy. But they are deeply involved in another cause that is their true passion. While they like you and know that you are doing good work, you are never going to make it to the top third of their giving list.

Let them go graciously. Thank them sincerely for taking their time to come. If they are open enough to mention the other issue or organization they are involved with, compliment it. Honor their commitment and dedication to that cause. Do not even offer to send them an envelope they can use to make a small gift. Let them completely off the hook. It will disarm them and distinguish you from the others. Think of how grateful you would feel if people heard you the first time when you really meant "No."

In the long run, these people will help you in many ways, primarily by referring others. Many times, people have told me, "This type of program just isn't my thing, I'm deeply involved in another organization, and that's where I want to be putting my resources right now." Then, when I asked them the final question about others they know who might want to come to a Point of Entry Event, they would often say, "You should definitely call my wife (or my work colleague or my friend). This is exactly the kind of thing they'd be interested in. Tell them I recommend they come out and take your tour." What better compliment than for a person to refer you to others and encourage you to use their name? In the long run, you will have made a real friend, just by letting someone off the hook.

Remember, this is a model for building lifelong donors—donors who are so interested in your mission that they want to stay with you. It's as if, one by one, you are selecting the people who are going to be part of your organization's family forever. You do not want to select someone who is not really interested. There are so many generous and caring folks who truly understand what you are doing. They are the ones you are on a scouting mission to find.

The Cultivation Superhighway

Where we are headed in the model is to the third step, where the donor is asked for money. Notice you have not done that at either Step One, the Point of Entry Event, or at Step Two, the Follow-Up Call. You have been busy warming up and screening people to see if they would make a loyal lifelong donor. In our model, by the time you get around to asking for money, you should be certain that the person is ready to give.

In the old reality, the "Ask" often happened right away, before the person had a chance to buy in, head and heart, to the mission of the organization. In the new reality, there is no need for that. In fact, if you have any question that the person may not be ready to give, don't ask yet. Trust your instincts and hold off until they are ready.

Asking is very much like picking the ripe, low-hanging fruit from a fruit tree. When a person first comes to your Point of Entry Event, they are brand new to your organization, completely unripened fruit. By taking them through the tour, they begin to ripen, and with the Follow-Up Call they ripen further. By the time you get around to asking them for money, it should be nothing more than "nudging the inevitable"—like easily picking a piece of fruit off a tree the moment it is ready. On the other hand, if you wait too long, what happens? The fruit becomes overripe, falls to the ground and spoils. In other words, in the life cycle of each donor, there are perfect moments for asking for money. You have to tune your radar to those moments.

In this model, everything between Step Two, the Follow-Up Call, and Step Three, the Ask, is called the Cultivation Superhighway. The more contacts you have with a potential donor along the Superhighway, the more money they will give you when you ask. There is a direct correlation between the number of contacts and the size of the gifts received.

THE CULTIVATION SUPERHIGHWAY

This should come as no surprise. Again, think of yourself as that donor. Imagine that an organization had already taken the time to educate you and follow up personally. The more you heard from a real person at that organization directly and the more specifically their calls, e-mails, faxes or meetings with you related to your specific needs, the more inclined you would be to give a larger gift the next time they asked.

It is worth considering what qualifies as a contact. Is it mailing a potential donor your newsletter or invitations to upcoming events? Yes, those count as contacts, but nothing substitutes for a person-to-person, live contact. The best of these contacts are dictated by the donor. If they are generous enough in the Follow-Up Call to tell you how they might like to become more involved, your job is to stay in contact with them to make those things happen. Keep following up; keep giving them feedback.

If, for example, they would like to help you start a new program you would love to have, you will need to invite them back to meet with the key staff in that area, with the board or the director. Or there may be other folks from the community that the potential donor would also like to involve. Having them invite others to find out about your organization at a Point of Entry Event is also a key indicator of their support.

If you have done your homework and tended to their needs and interests throughout all of your contacts with them, this person will become a self-proclaimed volunteer for your organization. While their "project" may not fit into your normal job description for a volunteer, in the new reality of raising funds from individuals this person is a volunteer with a customized, self-designed job description.

Eighty-four percent of all charitable contributions come from households in which one or more family members volunteer. In other words, being a volunteer is a key indicator of giving. While the research doesn't specify that volunteers give to the same organizations where they volunteer their time, it does show that giving follows involvement. And in the new reality of individual giving, you should assume that giving will follow involvement, in whatever way the donor defines involvement.

Donors need to know that you need them and that their contribution will make a difference in accomplishing your mission. They need to know that you are responsive to their suggestions. In many cases, they need to know that you need them for more than their money. The more meaningful the contacts, the better. Contacts are what ripen the fruit.

Step Three: Asking for Money

When the donor is ready to be asked, the first thing to consider is the medium you will use. Will you ask in person, over the telephone, online, at an event or by mail? Any of these is acceptable, although, generally speaking, the bigger the gift you will be asking for, the more successful you will be by asking face-to-face and one-on-one.

If you have taken many people through your Point of Entry in a short span of time, then followed up and involved them to their satisfaction, you may well find yourself in the enviable position of having many people to ask for a contribution at about the same time. In that case, the Free One-Hour Ask Event is ideal (see Chapter 16). The critical mass of true believers in the same room will produce breakthrough results in an hour.

On the other hand, if people have been trickling through your Point of Entry Events more slowly, or if you are starting with Points of Re-Entry for prior donors, you may do better asking one-on-one, in person or by phone. If your donors prefer online communication, this entire model can be implemented online, including the Ask.

Regardless of the medium or venue, in this model, every Ask must include two essential ingredients.

STEP THREE: **ASKING FOR MONEY**

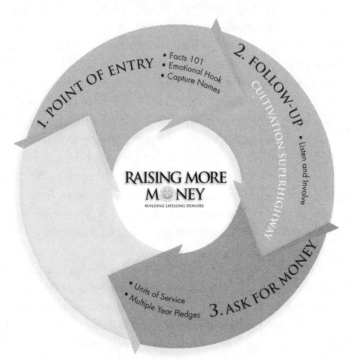

Multiple-Year Pledges

The first essential ingredient in asking for money is that you ask people to become part of a Multiple-Year Giving Society by making a multiple-year pledge to support the unrestricted operating needs of the organization. That's right, you ask them to commit at the time of their first pledge to give that same amount each year for a specified number of years. Why? Not for the reason you may think. As wonderful as it is for your organization to know you have the stability of all those pledges waiting to be collected each year, that is not the main reason for asking for multiple-year pledges.

The reason is for the donor. It allows donors to declare themselves as part of your organization's family. It gives a particular group of more committed donors the opportunity to say: "You can count on me. I'm a long-term believer in what you are up to."

Think for a moment about your own giving, that mental list you made earlier of all the places you have been supporting over the years, getting relatively little feedback in return. What if someone from that organization was to call you and say: "Hello, Ms. Jones, we notice you have been a loyal donor for the last fifteen years. Thank you for your support. We are calling to ask if you would be willing to make a pledge to give that same level of gift for the next five years." You would have a hard time saying no, right? After all, the odds are you will keep giving there indefinitely.

The value of a Multiple-Year Giving Society is that it allows donors to "go public" with their commitment and support. Most of us are very private in our giving. We just keep sending in our little (or not so little) check year after year. We aren't looking for any recognition. We each have our personal reasons for giving. We don't even talk about our giving with others. The satisfaction of giving is often more than enough.

By making a multiple-year pledge, we know that our name will be listed in the Multiple-Year Society. Others may notice. Moreover, it gives us license to talk about our fondness for this organization with those close to us—family and friends, the people we trust, respect and confide in. Our natural tendency as a person who has made that multiple-year commitment is to share our enthusiasm with others.

Units of Service

When asking for multiple-year pledges, specify the levels of contribution. We call these Units of Service. They are the giving levels, gift clubs—gimmicks, if you will. They are the bite-sized chunks of unrestricted funding that one person can support. They relate to the needs that were clearly identified at the Point of Entry Event and at every contact along the way.

You do not need more than three Units of Service, and there should be a significant gap in their dollar levels. In the new reality, the lowest level will be $1,000 a year (which averages out to $83 a month). Many people who truly love your organization and want to be lifelong members of your family can and will give at that level. In fact, many may already be giving at that level when you total up their many gifts each year.

The key thing to know is that these levels are gimmicks, and in the new reality of lifelong donors it is fine to tell people that. If they have bought into your mission fully, they will trust you to use the money for the overall programs of the organization. They know that someone has to pay the light bill and the salaries. They know they can look at your annual audit if they want to see exactly how the money was spent.

Step Four: Introducing Others; Reconnecting Existing Donors

This leads to the fourth step in our model where individual members of the Multiple-Year Giving Society introduce others to your organization by inviting them to a Point of Entry Event. Since they have been through the cycle with you, they know that you will take good care of their friends. You will educate and inspire them at the Point of Entry, follow up personally, involve them as appropriate or let them off the hook graciously if they are not interested. They trust the organization to treat their friends with respect. Their secret hope, of course, is that their friends will fall in love with your organization too—in their own right, for their own reasons—and become lifelong donors as well. This step completes the first circuit around the model for a brand-new donor.

STEP FOUR: **DONORS INTRODUCE OTHERS**

Free Feel-Good Cultivation Events: Points of Re-Entry

To keep your donors on the cycle, every Multiple-Year Giving Society donor is invited to two or three Free Feel-Good Cultivation Events during the year—also called Points of Re-Entry. As the name implies, these events serve to reconnect them to the facts and emotion of your work. Donors are encouraged to invite others to Free Feel-Good/Point of Re-Entry Events. For these new guests, this event will be their Point of Entry. For the prior donors, the event serves to reinforce their wise investment in your organization and to deepen their interest and commitment.

These Free Feel-Good Cultivation Events can be regularly scheduled events having to do with the work of the organization, such as a graduation of your program's participants or a lecture on a topic of interest. Or they can be events planned specially for these donors. You may even choose to have different events for donors at different levels.

Following each Free Feel-Good Cultivation/Point of Re-Entry Event, every donor receives another one-on-one Follow-Up Call, asking a few more open-ended questions, including suggestions for names of others to be invited to a Point of Entry Event. This in turn leads to more cultivation, more involvement, deeper and deeper permission or trust. Whatever they tell you in each Follow-Up Call determines the frequency and quality of involvement they would like to have, including the timing of the next Ask.

After the next gift is received, another Follow-Up Call is made to say thank you; there is more conversation, and on it goes. All the while you are looking and listening for how else they might want to become involved, inviting them to take on a leadership role, key volunteer or board position, as appropriate.

Ideally, in the course of the year, you have three or four occasions for personal, one-on-one contact with each donor. This contact can be made by your lead development staff person or other key staff or by one of your volunteer Donor Service Representatives (akin to a customer service representative in a bank) who is assigned to that donor for two years at a time. These contacts are nothing intrusive or artificial, but rather a natural give-and-take, either triggered by gifts received or by their participation in one of your Free Feel-Good Cultivation Events.

Thus, the simple circle becomes a spiral, with an ever-growing number of Multiple-Year Donors.

THE POINT OF ENTRY

CHAPTER 3

THE POINT OF ENTRY

Part of the legacy you want to leave for your organization is a brilliant Point of Entry—a powerful, succinct show-and-tell hour about your organization's fine work. That Point of Entry would be so generic, so easy to produce and so memorable, that it would live on forever as part of your organization's system for building lifelong donors. Furthermore, the elements of your Point of Entry are the same elements that will be needed as you customize the entire Raising More Money Model to your organization.

At the school in Seattle where this model was first implemented, our seemingly casual Thursday morning tours are still taking place like clockwork. All month long, as people call in to inquire about the school or as board members and volunteers come into contact with people who are interested in knowing more, they are invited to come to the tour next week. During the ten years since the tours began, thousands of people have attended these Point of Entry Events. The tours have become institutionalized as a normal part of day-to-day life at the school. They are part of a larger system that is not dependent on one charismatic development director. To this day, I still frequently run into people in Seattle who tell me enthusiastically, "I will never forget that tour." That's how memorable your Point of Entry has to be.

You do not need to be a school with adorable children to have a powerful Point of Entry. There is an ideal Point of Entry for every organization, regardless of your location, your size, or the type of work you do. This chapter will spell out the generic elements that will allow you to customize the Point of Entry to your organization.

The Point of Entry is the starting point in building your organization's self-sustaining cycle of individual giving. It is a one-hour, sizzling yet succinct introduction to your organization at the basic level. It must contain enough facts and emotion to make a lasting impact on each and every guest. No one is asked to give money at a Point of Entry Event. Because you should assume each donor will attend only one full-fledged Point of Entry Event in their lifetime, do your best to make it memorable!

You are aiming to design a generic Point of Entry program, one you can repeat easily and often. Remember, there are three essential ingredients every Point of Entry must include:

- The Facts about your organization
- The Emotional Hook
- Capturing the Names of each guest, with their permission

Without all three of these ingredients, you might have a nice event or gathering, but it will not be a Point of Entry.

FOCUS ON THE PROGRAM

The first question that people ask after they get interested in Points of Entry is where to have them—the venue. After working intensively to customize Points of Entry for each organization that comes through our workshops, we have seen that this is not the place to begin. Begin by designing the content of the program. Once the content and program are refined, they can be delivered in many venues and by using many media. The content can be scaled to groups as large as one hundred or one hundred and fifty or as small as one guest. The key is designing, practicing, testing and refining a succinct and powerful way to tell your organization's story in one hour or less. This can be a daunting challenge, especially if you complicate the process. Again, I encourage you to follow the formula and not get creative.

PROGRAM FORMAT

We will focus on the program first and then come back to look at possible venues, best times to hold your Points of Entry and all of the other questions people often ask.

Let's walk though each element of your one-hour program.

POINT OF ENTRY AGENDA

1. **Greeting**
2. **Sign In**
3. **Mix & Mingle**
4. **Program**
    a. **Welcome**
    b. **Visionary Leader Talk**
    c. **Facts**
    d. **Q & A**
    e. **Emotional Hook**
       • **Essential Story**
       • **Tour, Audio, Video, Live Testimonial**
    f. **Thank You/Wrap-Up**

Selecting Your "Cast"

For a full-scale Point of Entry, your cast will include the Host (a board member or volunteer), the Visionary Leader, and the development director or designated fundraising person who will be making the Follow-Up Call. You will want to make sure the follow-up person is prominently placed in the program so people will remember him or her. In addition, if your program includes a live testimonial from a staff member or a person who has benefited from your work, these people will need to be part of your cast.

Greeting

From the perspective of the guests, the Point of Entry Event begins as they arrive and are greeted at the door or even at the curb. In Seattle, for our rainy morning Point of Entry Events at a somewhat hard-to-find location, I would often stand out at the curb under an umbrella to greet people as they drove up. Be prepared to do whatever it takes to make your guests feel comfortable as they arrive.

Think about who will greet each of your visitors and where they will be stationed. Ideally, the greeter will be the person who invited them—friend, board member, etc. The next best choice is the development director or the person who will be their ongoing liaison with the organization. Note that you may want to save the executive director or chief executive officer for cameo roles later.

The greeter welcomes the guests, takes their coats and walks with them to the sign-in table.

Sign-In: Capturing Names with Permission

The Raising More Money Model is permission-based. By that we mean we must earn people's permission, incrementally, to proceed around the circle with them. Permission correlates with trust. To the extent that we trust someone, we give that person more permission. Conversely, to the extent that we stop trusting them, we take away our permission. In terms of our lifelong relationship with potential donors, this permission/trust is initially established at the Point of Entry.

The majority of your Point of Entry guests will have been invited to attend personally by a friend. They have been told that your organization is trying to spread the word in the community about its good work, and that you are looking for feedback about your work and how you are telling your story. They are told in advance that they will not be asked to give money at the Point of Entry Event.

Therefore, when they arrive that first day at the Point of Entry, they know that they are coming to a one-hour introductory event. They are coming to check out your work at the recommendation of a trusted friend. They are predisposed to like you. They are willing to give you their basic contact information.

The trust you are looking to establish begins at the moment you ask someone for their name and other contact information at the Point of Entry. If you use the outdated trick of asking them to put their business card in the bowl for a drawing, they know that you do your fundraising using manipulation and strong-arm tactics. Conversely, if you are straight with people as they sign in for your Point of Entry, they will know they are dealing with a straightforward, modern organization they can trust—one they might like to stay involved with.

The Sign-In Table

The sign-in table is the essential checkpoint through which all visitors must pass. A friendly, detail-oriented staff person or volunteer seated behind the table gives them a sign-in card and waits while they fill it out. The only information you have enough permission to gather at this early stage is their name, address, phone number (whichever one they want to give you), e-mail address and the name of the person who invited them to the Point of Entry Event. If guests ask what this is for, simply tell them that you would like to call them to follow up and get their feedback about the event.

If you have enough guests to warrant it, nametags should be provided at the sign-in table as well.

Brief Mix-and-Mingle Time

As the rest of the guests are gathering, offer them a cup of coffee or tea, if appropriate, and introduce them to other visitors. This is a good time for the executive director to enter and be available for informal conversations. Point out pictures on the walls, displays, scrapbooks or any key features of the room they are in.

Guests Are Seated

Everyone is seated. This is critical. Do not ever attempt to have a Point of Entry Event if people are standing up (unless, of course, they are walking around on a tour). If you want them to focus, give them a seat. At their place, waiting for them, is a packet of handouts that outline general information about your organization and your area of work.

Program Content
Welcome

The program begins with a welcome greeting from the board member or volunteer who is hosting the Point of Entry Event, or, in their absence, the most senior fund development staff member present. This person should take a moment to tell how they became involved with the organization.

The Visionary Leader Talk

Every organization has a Visionary Leader. Generally this is the executive director or founder, if the founder is still active in the daily operations of the organization.

The Visionary Leader Talk generally lasts five to ten minutes. It tells people about the past, present and future of the organization, with emotion.

Most Visionary Leaders are very passionate people, yet when asked to speak about their organizations, many Visionary Leaders default to what they think people want to hear: a professional, clinical listing of the programs and services of the organization. Your Visionary Leader must convey how the organization got started, where you are now and where you are headed. They must make it clear to the guests that they see clearly where you are going and that they need support from the community in order to get there. In other words, they must convey a clear sense of "the gap," as well as their plan, even loosely defined, for filling that gap. And they must do this with genuine emotion.

VISIONARY LEADER TALK

I. **Brief history of the organization**
    - When was it founded?
    - By whom?
    - How has it evolved and grown since then?

II. **Mission and underlying philosophy**
    - Why does the organization really exist?
    - What values does it teach, encourage or represent?

III. **Top three programs and services offered**

    What is the simplest way to categorize/cluster your programs so a new person can understand what you do? (Do not try to include all programs in the list.) What programs might people be least aware of?

IV. **"Myth-buster" statistics**
    - How many people does your organization serve or reach?
    - How does that population differ from what people would expect?
    - How big is your budget? What are the biggest expense categories?
    - Where does your funding come from? (Show a pie chart or other graphic representation of your funding picture.)

V. **The gap**
    - What will it take for you to fulfill your mission?
    - How many people are unserved or underserved now?
    - What is the impact to society of the absence of those needed programs and services?

VI. **A story**
    - What keeps you working there?
    - What one story always reconnects you to the importance of your work?

VII. Vision for the future

- **Where do you want to be five to ten years from now?**
- **How much closer to fulfilling that mission will you be?**
- **How many more people will benefit?**
- **What is the simple overview of your plan for getting there?**

Questions and Answers

At the end of this informational segment of the Point of Entry Event, the person who will be making the Follow-Up Calls to each guest asks for questions. This positions the speaker as knowledgeable. Allow time for three or four questions. Invite those with more questions to stay after the meeting to talk further.

The Emotional Hook

The second essential ingredient at a Point of Entry is the Emotional Hook. Remember that, as individuals, we are first and foremost emotional donors. We justify our emotional decision to give with the facts. Assuming this will be the one and only Point of Entry for each guest, your Emotional Hook has got to move them.

The true Emotional Hook for your organization, as we will see in Chapter 5, is a complex mix of the emotions, values, stereotypes and dreams your work stirs up in people. This "internal" Emotional Hook may not be something you ever say out loud. It is the deeper, compelling, instinctive feeling that moves people to jump in and take action. At your Point of Entry Event, you definitely want to stir up this internal Emotional Hook, while at the same time demonstrating the more obvious, "external" Emotional Hooks, such as the cute kids or the hard-working families, either by meeting these people firsthand or through testimonials, a video, or stories.

In the old fundraising reality, our foremost concern was protecting the privacy and dignity of our clients, families, children, artists, etc. We were so focused on not wanting to exploit anyone's situation that we went overboard in the other direction. We consciously avoided eliciting any emotion about our work. We wanted to be very professional. Fundraising became almost clinical. Is it any wonder we now find ourselves in the world of special events that deflect attention from the real mission of the organization?

In the new fundraising reality, this seems ridiculous. If we assume people naturally want to get involved in our work, why would we withhold the core of it? Wouldn't we want them to know the facts about child abuse? Wouldn't we want them to hear a firsthand testimonial from a former client, family member, or staff member, presented in an appropriate manner? Wouldn't we want them to hear directly from a rural villager about the impact of that environmental issue on his family?

The Emotional Hook answers the question: How does the work of this organization impact the life of one individual? How does it affect real people? Whether your mission is related to saving whales or saving orphans, the fundraising dollars you are looking for are going to come from real people—people with a pre-existing frame of reference: themselves. They will be asking themselves: How does this really work? How much of an impact does this really have on one ordinary person like me? How important is it to me that this problem be solved?

Do not be afraid to use emotion. Today's donors are hungry for it. They are counting on you to inspire them. In fact, many would say that in our "high-tech" world, "high touch" is more valued than ever. Your organization offers your donors high touch. Don't hold back on using it. And keep it simple. Your goal is to provide an experience and paint a picture in people's minds—an indelible picture. It needs to move them to tears.

The easiest way to provide an Emotional Hook for guests at your Point of Entry is through stories. People will remember a story. You need to decide as an organization what your one "Essential Story" is. Then you can choose the ideal medium by which to convey this story.

The Essential Story

The Essential Story is the archetypal story that always conveys the emotional essence of your work. It may be a composite of several stories woven together, but they are stories of real people whose lives have been changed, thanks to your organization. It moves you every time you tell it. Perhaps it is the story of the abandoned child, the person who beat the odds, the family that got back on their feet, thanks to your organization. It may be the story of the family in the rainforest or of one of the lives saved as a result of your organization's work to remove land mines.

Whatever the Essential Story for your organization, everyone involved agrees that it conveys the essence of your work powerfully each time that story is told. What is your organization's Essential Story?

Ways to Communicate the Essential Story

Once you know the Essential Story, you can use any or all of the following elements to tell it. Keep it brief and to the point.

TOUR: Let people see your compelling work firsthand. Intersperse each stop on the tour with anecdotes. You are painting a picture as you walk people through the building. Keep highlighting the needs. Even if all you have to tour is your standard office, you can set up stations in each work area with photos and stories of people served. Have two or three staff members prepared to give a testimonial story of someone they will never forget. Their passion for their work, combined with the gripping stories and surrounded by photos, will move and inspire your visitors.

VIDEO: Another way to communicate the Emotional Hook is to use a video. While this is not necessary at the Point of Entry, if you decide to make a video, consider any video footage you may already have before launching into a costly production. A brief news clip about your organization, clarified with verbal remarks to put it in context and add the missing points, can be excellent. If you are part of a national organization, check to see what generic video material is available to you. You might even excerpt a portion of the national material and combine it with your local story.

If you want to make a new video, try to get it donated or get special funding to produce it. Consider hiring a producer who has worked in television news. They are experts at painting a succinct emotional picture with images, words and music that both educate and move the audience. For more details on making a video, see Chapter 22.

LIVE TESTIMONIALS: There is no substitute for the live testimonial. Having the person tell their own story right there at your Point of Entry can be extremely compelling—assuming the testimonial speaker is having a good day. It can also drag on too long with too much or too little emotion. If you are planning to have the same testimonial speaker at each of your Points of Entry, consider their availability as well as their skill at telling their story consistently each time.

The outline for the ideal testimonial talk is quite simple. It covers the following questions, in sequence:

1. What my life was like before.

2. I decided to make a change and found this wonderful organization.

3. Now my life is so much better, for example: _____ .

4. Now I'm more committed than ever to helping others in the same situation I was in by doing _____ .

AUDIOTAPE: Another highly effective medium for communicating your Essential Story at the Point of Entry Event is audiotape. It has the added benefits of being inexpensive to produce and easy to transport, while offering the immediacy of voice and sound. Many groups, especially those who feel they have "boring office syndrome" do very well with audiotape. These can be combined with a tour by having a different audiotaped testimonial or story to be played at several points along the office tour.

LETTERS: Testimonials in the form of letters are also very powerful, especially if they are read by someone who knows or knew the person who wrote the letter. A simple letter of thanks to a caring staff member, with details of how the person's life was changed thanks to the organization, can be very moving. These also work well in confidential situations and where the Point of Entry will be moved to many remote locations.

PHOTOS: If it is true that a picture conveys a thousand words, what better way to tell your story? Whether through a photo album on the table or large blown-up photos posted on the walls, do consider using photos at your Point of Entry. Sometimes the addition of a caption or quote from the person in the photo can add that extra tug at the heartstrings.

Thank You and Wrap-Up

Be sure you conclude on time. If the last segment of your Point of Entry Event is the tour, end by bringing the group back to the front door. Thank them for taking their time to come. Let them know you would like to call them in the next week to get their feedback and advice.

I do not recommend doing a group debriefing or group feedback session at the end. One person's feedback or complaint may never have occurred to the others and may only serve to distract and confuse your happy guests. There will be plenty of time for debriefing your guests one-on-one during the Follow-Up Call.

OTHER FACTORS TO CONSIDER

Let's look at the individual components that make up a successful and memorable Point of Entry Event.

The Venue

Most often, the Point of Entry will be an event, a gathering of real people in real time, to learn about your program. The classic Point of Entry Event is a tour. If your organization lends itself at all to a tour, this should definitely be your preferred Point of Entry.

Even if you think there would not be much for people to see at your office, there is a lot you can do to spice it up and turn it into the perfect venue for a Point of Entry Event. You can add photos to the walls and tell a story about what goes on in each room as you walk people through. Stopping by the desk of a hard-working staff person to have them share an anecdote about a child or adult who has benefited from their program will make a big impact, as will showing an outstanding video or having someone read a testimonial in your conference room.

If you are concerned about the confidential nature of what people might see on a tour, there are ways to highlight only the programs or clients you want them to see. Many excellent Points of Entry have been done in one room only, without ever walking people through the facility. By using video, photos, audiotaped and live testimonials, you can paint a powerful picture that people will never forget. If your organization has a site or an office, people will feel more connected to your organization, and they will remember you best if they have physically been to your site. Chapter 11 will detail the classic in-office Point of Entry Event.

If you conclude you cannot have an on-site tour, here are some other examples of venues for Points of Entry:

- A box-lunch at a board member's office
- Evening "house parties" in people's homes
- A one-on-one meeting anywhere
- An alumni gathering in each of your regions or cities
- An online Point of Entry Event
- A self-contained Point of Entry mailer that includes a video, a written testimonial letter, and a list of questions for discussion

Ideal Size

The ideal size for a regularly scheduled on-site Point of Entry is somewhere between ten and fifteen people. This allows for personal interaction and a manageable follow-up schedule.

Having said that, there are many exceptions. One large university medical research institution puts on a major high-end Point of Entry half-day event once a year. Tightly choreographed and held on a Saturday morning, this event educates and inspires one hundred and fifty guests. All guests attend the President's Visionary Leader Talk before being divided into smaller groups (pre-selected by the guests) where medical researchers each present the Facts 101 and the Emotional Hook about their respective research. The morning concludes with a lovely lunch back in the larger group, allowing for the sharing of ideas among guests. Guests are guided through the half-day process by the staff member who will be their ongoing liaison to the organization.

At the other extreme, your Point of Entry does not need to be done in a group at all. You could do a One-on-One Point of Entry with a person sitting next to you on an airplane or standing next to you in a long line. It doesn't have to take a long time. We will talk more about the One-on-One Point of Entry in Chapter 10.

Timing

Your full Point of Entry should last one hour—no longer.

Deciding when to have your Point of Entry Events takes experimentation and depends on where they will be held. Your first consideration should be what time is most convenient for your guests. If you are asking them to come to an out-of-the-way location, what time of day is easiest for them to get there? Working people might prefer early morning or late in the day or lunchtime, especially if you offer a light lunch as part of the Point of Entry. Stay-at-home parents and retired people may prefer midday.

Next, consider the best time to show them your programs or take them on your tour. If you are planning to include live testimonials from staff or program participants, what times of day are those programs in session? Even within the work day, there may be certain times when there is more to see than others; for example, times when the kids are the freshest or the volunteers are busiest. Many arts organizations will hold their Points of Entry in conjunction with a rehearsal or preview showing, which dictates the best dates and times. This is often the case with Points of Re-Entry, such as an alumni weekend reunion, which we will discuss further in Chapter 17.

Do not overlook evenings and weekends as good times to hold your Point of Entry Events. Those times work best for many people. For example, a faith-based retirement home holds their Points of Entry on Sundays at lunchtime, which is when family members usually come to visit their elderly parents and grandparents. Many Habitat for Humanity affiliates put on their Points of Entry on Saturdays at lunch, in conjunction with their home building. That is the time when their morning volunteers and afternoon volunteers overlap and take a break. Weeknights in people's living rooms often work well for grass-roots and women's organizations.

Naming Your Point of Entry

Take the time to choose a clever, inviting name for your Point of Entry. The term "Point of Entry" is for your internal use only. It is much too clinical to use with the general public.

One Raising More Money Workshop participant team from an organ-donor program named their Point of Entry Events "Lifesaver Events." One Red Cross chapter named theirs "The Red Cross Experience." Other groups call their names such as "Meet Family Services," "Getting to Know Your Humane Society," or "Village Theater 101," or even something as generic as "Tuesday Tours." One organization that serves abused children calls their Points of Entry "If These Walls Could Talk." A Girl Scout council calls theirs "Beyond the Cookie Box." Find something unique and clever that reflects your mission in some way.

Handouts at Your Point of Entry

Do not overwhelm people at Point of Entry Events with printed materials. When they arrive, have the following three items waiting at their places at the table:

1. Your Basic Brochure

It does not need to be your slickest five-color version. The basic model will do. As you launch your Point of Entry program, it is probably a good idea to reread your brochure from the perspective of the many new people who will be seeing it for the first time. While I certainly am not recommending you redesign and reprint your brochures, the Point of Entry process will help you test your existing printed material and modify it if necessary when it comes time to reprint.

In other words, will your brochure withstand the scrutiny of many new people? Does it convey quickly what your organization does? Does it use vocabulary that is understandable to a person not familiar with your field? Is it graphically interesting or too crammed full of text? Does it contain compelling photographs demonstrating your work?

Your brochure needs to be an engaging stand-alone piece that your enthusiastic Point of Entry guests will want to share with others.

2. The Fact Sheet

After you have had a few Point of Entry Events, the questions people need answered most often will become obvious. That is the time to make up a Fact Sheet. For your first Points of Entry, list the basic facts about your history, mission, purpose, as well as facts about your cause and the services you provide.

The Fact Sheet should be no more than one side of one page. It is not intended to be a substitute for your basic brochure. It should contain five or six key points about your services. Most likely, you will not have space to mention all of your programs. While each program seems essential to you, your guests do not need that level of detail. Figure out a way to cluster your programs and explain them simply. Have the information on the Fact Sheet follow the format you will be using at the Point of Entry Event. That way you can walk your guests right through the Fact Sheet as you go.

Just like your brochure, your Fact Sheet should also be inviting to the reader. You may want to use a question and answer format. Allow plenty of white space. Graphics are good. For example, you could include a pie chart about your budget or programs. The beauty of a one-page homemade Fact Sheet is you can change it easily. As you tune in to the questions people ask repeatedly, you can modify it. Consider your Fact Sheet a work in progress—just like your organization. (See Sample Fact Sheet in Chapter 4.)

3. The Wish List

The Wish List is an essential handout at a Point of Entry Event. Do not overlook it. It should include a wide assortment of needs, from Band-Aids to science laboratories. Take the time to interview your staff to develop a list of real items they would love to have. You can cluster the items by program (the preschool's Wish List, the high school's Wish List) or any other subgroup (the teachers' list, the students' list, the administration's list). Make the items personal: cooking supplies for a family of four, a computer and workstation for an elementary school classroom. There should be no price tags on the Wish List. Just list the items—small, medium and large.

The simple Wish List is a powerful tool for engaging people in a nonthreatening way with your organization. It lets people know where they can fit in and contribute right away. People will glance at the Wish List during your Point of Entry Event program. In the Follow-Up Call, when you ask people if there is any way they could see themselves becoming involved with your organization, many people will refer back to an item they saw listed on the Wish List that they have to contribute.

As you begin to receive the items on your list, be sure to update the Wish List regularly to keep it fresh. You can even make a new version of your Wish List for the holiday season or other special events or special times of year.

SAMPLE: WISH LIST

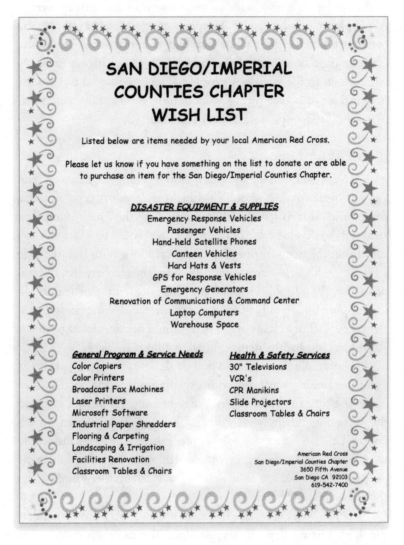

SAN DIEGO/IMPERIAL COUNTIES CHAPTER WISH LIST

Listed below are items needed by your local American Red Cross.

Please let us know if you have something on the list to donate or are able to purchase an item for the San Diego/Imperial Counties Chapter.

DISASTER EQUIPMENT & SUPPLIES

Emergency Response Vehicles
Passenger Vehicles
Hand-held Satellite Phones
Canteen Vehicles
Hard Hats & Vests
GPS for Response Vehicles
Emergency Generators
Renovation of Communications & Command Center
Laptop Computers
Warehouse Space

General Program & Service Needs

Color Copiers
Color Printers
Broadcast Fax Machines
Laser Printers
Microsoft Software
Industrial Paper Shredders
Flooring & Carpeting
Landscaping & Irrigation
Facilities Renovation
Classroom Tables & Chairs

Health & Safety Services

30" Televisions
VCR's
CPR Manikins
Slide Projectors
Classroom Tables & Chairs

American Red Cross
San Diego/Imperial Counties Chapter
3650 Fifth Avenue
San Diego CA 92103
619-542-7400

(American Red Cross, San Diego/Imperial Counties Chapter)

THE POINT OF ENTRY IN A BOX

Whatever the venue and timing of your Points of Entry, they must be easy for you to conduct on a regular basis. The more often you change locations or hosts or time of day, the more you complicate things for yourself. Keep it simple. At the school where this model was developed, once we got our Point of Entry Event format refined, we were conducting breakfast tours as often as three times a week. I could arrive at the school, take out my Point of Entry box—complete with name tags, sign-in sheets, handouts, pens, brochures and other supplies—and set up the event in half an hour.

After you have designed, tested and refined your Points of Entry over time, they should become almost routine to you. You may find yourself dreading yet another Point of Entry Event. Once the program begins, however, you will become drawn in by the compelling facts and emotional stories, and just like your guests, you will be inspired.

At this point, the program elements will have become repeatable and generic. Even if your testimonial speaker is unable to attend, you have a backup method of conveying the same story or message. If your board member has to cancel at the last minute, someone else from the team can stand in and welcome the guests. The entire program becomes so familiar, it is almost as if you could—figuratively speaking—put the program elements in a box and take it on the road. You could take it to a board member's office or conference room, a volunteer's living room or a church basement. We call this generic Point of Entry your "Point of Entry in a Box." It is what you are aiming for if you are interested in leaving the Point of Entry system as a legacy for your organization.

CHAPTER 4

THE FACTS 101

Zeroing in on which basic facts to convey at your Point of Entry can be complicated. It is worth taking the time to sort through your options before selecting the key facts you will use. You can then find opportunities to integrate these facts seamlessly into many parts of the Point of Entry program.

YOU NEED A FOCUS

In the process of designing a generic Point of Entry, sooner or later most organizations ask the question: How do we explain the facts about so many different programs? The answer is: you don't.

Remember that the one-hour sizzling event you are designing is a Point of *Entry*. It is only the beginning of a lifelong relationship with someone who is checking out your work to see if they would like to become involved and learn more. There will be plenty of time later to tell them about all your programs in detail.

To boil down your organization's work to a short presentation means that you will have to synthesize the common elements of your work for people and highlight only a few examples of your programs.

Point 1: List Your Programs

Start by making a standard list of all the programs you offer. You know this list well. Yet to most newcomers to your organization, this list will be overwhelming and confusing, filled with jargon. To them, it may sound vague and redundant. While you may think it is essential to tell the world about even the sub-levels of programs you offer in your many geographically dispersed sites, they are not ready to absorb all of that information yet. Giving people too much information can make them feel slow or stupid and they will want to back off from being more involved with you. Instead, I recommend you again zero in.

Point 2: Summarize Your Work

Looking back over your list of all of your programs, what few sentences best summarize all of your work? Here is an example from a complex multiple-service program for Brazilian orphans: "We serve orphans in Brazil. We provide many of the essential services the children need to become healthy, successful adults. From basic food and housing to health care, education and spiritual development, we become their surrogate family until they are eighteen years old, and sometimes beyond that."

Point 3: Tell Your Story

Then, tell your story using testimonials, videos and letters, combined with a powerful Fact Sheet displaying the statistics about the need for what you offer. In the case of the program for Brazilian orphans, their Fact Sheet listed each of their programs by name as well as the number of children served by that program each year. Of course, they also had statistics about the number of children they had to turn away.

Imagine yourself as a guest at their Point of Entry Event. Rather than leaving overwhelmed and confused by too much detail, you are inspired and motivated to become involved. There were just enough facts provided so that you could see where you might fit in. Whether you were a teacher, a health care practitioner, a parent, a real estate person, or a restaurant owner, there was something to pull at your heartstrings and call you to action.

TOP THREE FREQUENTLY ASKED QUESTIONS

Begin by making a list of the three most frequently asked questions about your organization and how it affects everyday life for real people. These are usually not the questions you wish they would ask about the loftier issues you may be grappling with day to day. These are the threshold-level questions people need answered just to sort out how to categorize your organization within their frame of reference. You may want to brainstorm a list of these questions with your core staff, volunteers and board. As a take-off on the popular computer training books, you could call these questions "XYZ Organization for Dummies." This is not to imply that your guests are stupid, but merely that without having answers to these most basic questions, they will not be oriented to the work of your organization.

To use our inner-city school example again, the most frequently asked questions were: "How many students attend the school?" "What grades does the school cover?" "How much is the tuition?" "How are students referred to the school?" This is what I mean by basic questions. Of course some people asked more complex and probing questions, but these simple questions were the ones *most frequently asked.*

Now, in answering these questions, you can merely provide the short and simple answer, or you can use the opportunity to highlight little-known information about your programs or the people you serve. That way, in the context of answering a seemingly simple question, you are educating people and breaking down their stereotypes without insulting them. You are intertwining facts with one or more elements of the Emotional Hook.

For example, in response to the question about how students were referred to the school, we developed the following answer after much experimentation: "Most students just show up at our front door, having heard about the school from a friend. At least half of our kindergarten class arrives for the first time each year in November or December, accompanied by an angry and distraught parent whose child has been having difficulty in the public school system." Simple question, educational answer.

SAMPLE FAQ: CENTER SERVING HOMELESS STREET YOUTH

1. How big is this problem in our community?

2. How do street youth survive during the day and at night?

3. It seems like these kids will never get their lives together. What services do you provide that actually work?

TOP THREE FACTS

Once you have made your list of the most frequently asked questions, zero in on the top three little-known facts or statistics that showcase the importance of your work and help to answer these questions. These will be the three facts you will be certain to include in every Point of Entry. As you will see from the chilling facts from one sexual assault organization that participated in our Raising More Money Workshop recently, the facts are directly tied to the Emotional Hook. Simple facts can evoke powerful emotions.

TOP THREE FACTS: SEXUAL ASSAULT CENTER

1. There are ten cases of sexual assault reported every day right here in our community. Of those, we are able to serve only two new clients per day. We have to turn away the others who request services.

2. Last year we served approximately 1,200 women, men and children here in our community.

3. Last year, our oldest client was 86 and our youngest was nine months old.

Another way to arrive at the Top Three Facts for your organization is to consider the myths and stereotypes people have about your work. Each myth can be dispelled with a powerful statistic. A group serving street youth knew that the stereotypes of lazy, drug-addicted, dangerous kids might be dispelled by the statistics about the numbers of street youth who had been abused by their family members and felt life on the streets to be a safer alternative than life at home.

Do not underestimate the power of the facts and statistics. While these facts may seem familiar and elementary to you, remember that we are emotional donors looking for rational reasons to justify our emotional decisions to give. You must give people compelling facts and statistics to emphasize the actual need for your work.

Finally, do not feel limited by the facts you choose. Your guests will have time to ask questions during the Question and Answer section of your Point of Entry program. Eventually, after you have done your first ten or fifteen Points of Entry and listened carefully to the questions people ask, as well as tracking additional questions people may ask during the Follow-Up Call, you will figure out the best way to convey the facts on your Fact Sheet.

The Fact Sheet

Now that you have focused on the facts you want to highlight, you should put them into a one-page Fact Sheet. This can be done as a simple listing of facts with bullet points, charts and graphs, or a frequently asked questions fact sheet in question-and-answer format. As with everything else about the Point of Entry system, you will want to test out your fact sheet over time, constantly editing and streamlining the information. Eventually you will refine it to perfection.

SAMPLE: **FACT SHEET**

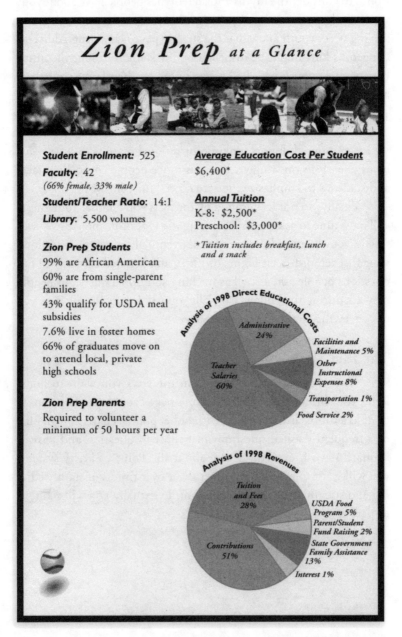

Zion Prep at a Glance

Student Enrollment: 525

Faculty: 42
(66% female, 33% male)

Student/Teacher Ratio: 14:1

Library: 5,500 volumes

Zion Prep Students

99% are African American

60% are from single-parent families

43% qualify for USDA meal subsidies

7.6% live in foster homes

66% of graduates move on to attend local, private high schools

Zion Prep Parents

Required to volunteer a minimum of 50 hours per year

Average Education Cost Per Student

$6,400*

Annual Tuition

K-8: $2,500*
Preschool: $3,000*

Tuition includes breakfast, lunch and a snack

Analysis of 1998 Direct Educational Costs

- Administrative 24%
- Facilities and Maintenance 5%
- Teacher Salaries 60%
- Other Instructional Expenses 8%
- Transportation 1%
- Food Service 2%

Analysis of 1998 Revenues

- Tuition and Fees 28%
- USDA Food Program 5%
- Parent/Student Fund Raising 2%
- Contributions 51%
- State Government Family Assistance 13%
- Interest 1%

(Zion Preparatory Academy, Seattle, WA)

CHAPTER 5

THE EMOTIONAL HOOK

Of the three key ingredients for a Point of Entry Event—the Facts 101, the Emotional Hook, and a system for Capturing the Names of your guests—the Emotional Hook is the golden nugget. Without it, you will never develop lifelong donors.

As I mentioned previously, individuals are emotional donors looking for rational reasons to justify their emotional decision to give. So if someone comes to your Point of Entry Event and you dazzle them with the facts alone, they probably won't be moved enough to give. They will lump your organization in with all the other nonprofits doing good work. They may walk away impressed and even a bit inspired, but they are not likely to be hooked. All the facts in the world cannot get us to give our biggest gift.

The guests who are coming to your Point of Entry Events are already predisposed to being moved and inspired by your work. They are hungry for ways to connect emotionally. Futurist Rolf Jensen says, "As information and intelligence become the domain of computers, society will place new value on the one human ability that can't be automated: emotion." Consumers are looking for outlets that provide "emotional jogging; they want to give their feelings a workout by using products and services that satisfy their desire to feel and display emotion."

There are very few legitimate outlets for emotion in our culture. Sporting events and sad movies come to mind. A direct exposure to the meaningful work of the nonprofit world is another. You have to be certain that your Point of Entry Event pulls at their heartstrings. If you only give them the standard, clinical presentation that people are accustomed to, they will sense it right away. You want them to know from the minute they walk up to the front door that this place is different. The Emotional Hook tells them that you really mean it about your mission. It tells you are absolutely passionate about your work.

You will need to model that passion for them. Passion is what they want from your Point of Entry Event. It is okay to rant and rave a little. Let them know what you stand for. Perhaps even share a personal story about why you are doing the work you are doing. Most of all, you want your guests to leave knowing what moves and motivates you about your work. If you can connect them to that passion, you will have gotten the job done.

Your job then is to figure out the Emotional Hook for your organization and to integrate it responsibly into every single communication your organization has with friends and donors, beginning with the Point of Entry Event. You need to be a walking Emotional Hook for people. Most of your organization's supporters will not wake up each morning thinking about your good work. You will be their reminder, their trigger. Once they have been to your Point of Entry Event, they will be counting on you to reconnect them to those same powerful emotions you triggered the first time.

Do you know what those emotions are? Can you summon them up for yourself, at any moment, to ensure that every donor or potential donor who comes in contact with you will be guaranteed a dose of that Emotional Hook?

EVERY ORGANIZATION HAS AN EMOTIONAL HOOK

Some of you may be concerned that your organization doesn't have such a hook. After all, you are doing broad-based policy work in an obscure area, several layers removed from the grass-roots level. People don't really understand your work, let alone become emotional about it. Do not worry. Whether your organization is a national or international think tank, a scientific professional association, or a children's hospital, every single nonprofit organization has an Emotional Hook.

PASSION RETREAD: TELL YOUR STORY

A good place to begin looking for your Emotional Hook is by asking yourself what got you involved with your organization in the first place. Whether you started there because you needed a job or because you were certain this was your life's work, at some point along the way, you became hooked.

It is worth looking at your story, or better yet, telling your story. In the work we do with people in our workshops to reveal the Emotional Hook of their organization, we start this "passion retread" work with the staff and volunteers.

For those who work day-to-day on the front lines, what seems like being emotionally cold or dispassionate may be natural self-preservation. At a training session for executive directors of fifty sexual assault and domestic violence organizations where we were refining the Emotional Hook, people spoke in jargon and abbreviations. When I asked them to define their terms, I was speechless. "These kinds of things actually happen to people? To children?" I stuttered. "Absolutely unthinkable."

They were concerned that if they zeroed in on their Emotional Hook, it would mean they would have to reveal confidential information. "All you have to do is define one of those terms, without ever mentioning a client's name," I said, "and people will get the message." Having them share their own stories about why they worked in this field was powerful. It returned them to their passion for their work that, understandably in many cases, had been buried for years.

Similarly, a professional association of scientists, seemingly interested only in statistics, formulas, and experiments, came alive when translating their passion for their work into a simplified, layperson's language I could understand. In several cases they were moved to tears by telling their stories of how they came to work in this field and what keeps them so engaged.

One group of hospital development staff I coached was getting ready to launch their biggest annual campaign ever. For several of the staff members, it would be their tenth or even twentieth annual campaign with this organization. They were hardened to the realities of life during campaign time and already dreading it. We put aside the agenda for our session and instead went around the room, with each person telling the story of how they had come to work at this organization in the first place. It was incredibly moving. They had never done this before. In the space of an hour, the entire mood altered. One by one, you could see them "reenlist" for the campaign, renewed and re-energized, ready to go.

This also works well for long-standing board and volunteers. It is a great exercise at retreats and planning sessions. It does not need to be overly gushy. Just have people tell their stories. It will reconnect them to their larger reasons for being there. It is a terrific lead-in exercise to customizing the Emotional Hook for your organization. If what you are after is to connect people to their own emotional response to your work, you have got to start by being reconnected to what hooks you about it. If you are not moved, how can you expect anyone else to be?

DISCOVERING AND CUSTOMIZING YOUR ORGANIZATION'S EMOTIONAL HOOK

The Emotional Hook for your organization may be more subtle than you expect. It is not a tag line, an icon or a logo. It is the rallying cry and driving force behind your organization, what really stirs people up about your cause. You may never say it out loud, yet it is the underpinning of everything you say.

The Emotional Hook we are after here is not the more obvious "external hook" you talk about openly when you tell your Essential Story: the sick child, the substance-abusing mom. That Essential Story is the tip of the iceberg of a much deeper and more complex swirl of emotions. We say it is made up of five elements, like the pieces of a pie. Each piece is something you may never say out loud, yet you need to include it, either directly or indirectly, at your Point of Entry.

COMPONENTS OF
THE EMOTIONAL HOOK

The elements of the Emotional Hook are:

1. The basic human emotions most stirred up by your work

2. The cherished cultural values, rights and ideals your organization addresses

3. People's deeply held negative stereotypes about your work or the people you serve

4. People's hopes and dreams for how much better the world would be if the mission of your organization were fulfilled

5. What you would tell people if you could look them in the eye and tell them straight about the real needs of the population you serve or your organization's mission

Let's examine each of these critical components one by one.

Basic Human Emotions

Think of the most basic human feelings, both positive and negative: fear, anger, sadness, joy, guilt, grief, hope, pity. These emotions are fundamental. They are usually stirred up before we ever speak of them. They can incite us to take action.

Fear can be one of the most powerful of these emotions: Fear of what kind of water my grandchildren and great-grandchildren will be drinking, fear of contracting a particular disease, fear of someone harming me or my family. And don't overlook guilt or pity. It is fairly safe to assume that once people learn the facts about your work or the statistics of the incidence of your issue, they will feel guilty for not having known those facts, done more about the issue, or even cared. Before they have time to read your brochure and tell you their response, they are feeling embarrassed and guilty about their ignorance.

Remember, these are not things you will ever say out loud. Merely being aware that your organization elicits these emotions in people will make you much more effective in your fundraising. You will want to make sure that your Point of Entry Events trigger those emotions every time, without leaving people feeling they have been manipulated. These deeper emotions, if triggered at your Point of Entry, will inspire many guests to take action.

Cherished Cultural Values, Rights, and Ideals

Think about the services your organization provides and the people who ultimately benefit from your work. Which closely held, cherished cultural values, rights and ideals does your work stir up in people?

For example, if your organization provides a range of services to homeless children, some of the values would be the value of a safe and healthy childhood, a family, a home, and education. If you work in the health care field, you are stirring up our cultural ideal of living a long, healthy life, the ideal that says no sick person should be turned away from a hospital, the value that says parents have a responsibility to take care of their children.

If you work in the area of domestic violence, you are dealing with people's values about safety, the rights of women and children, the value of family. In international relief work, you are dealing with the value that says those who have plenty should help those who have less, the value that says people deserve a chance for a better life. Other rights an organization's work might trigger are the right to privacy, to religious freedom, to education, and so on.

These are values we take for granted. They are so much a part of our way of life, we may not normally think about them. Yet, if one of those values is tampered with, we become deeply disturbed. "It is not right" that children are treated like that. "It is unthinkable" that in a society like ours, certain conditions still prevail. Take the time to consider what cherished cultural values, rights and ideals your organization deals with.

Stereotypes

Look at the issues or population your organization or program deals with. What are the bleakest stereotypes people have about "those kinds of people" or those issues?

To get started, just read through the list below and notice the stereotypes that immediately come to mind:

- Homeless men
- Homeless women
- Homeless children
- Suburban kids with learning disabilities
- Inner-city kids with learning disabilities
- Orphans in Brazil
- Baby girls in China
- Environmentalists
- Symphony orchestra
- Art museum board
- Political campaign reform
- World hunger
- Earthquake survivors
- New York City
- California
- Government employees
- High-tech entrepreneurs
- Private schools
- Debate club
- Hockey team

Our stereotypes are lying around dormant, waiting to be triggered by the mere thought of your issue or the population you are committed to serving.

The best way to zero in on the stereotypes people associate with your organization is to get a group of "outsiders" to help you paint the bleakest scenario possible. Most people think they already know the worst. In fact, there is usually more to know.

People, even good people like us, have some pretty nasty stereotypes that underlie our actions. Take, for example, homeless "street" youth. The list of stereotypes is long: scary, worthless, wasted lives, it's their own fault, drug addicts, prostitutes, drop-outs, dangerous, and so on. Our stereotypes call forth our smaller, petty selves. They are loaded with "shoulds." They allow us to justify the problem by saying: "They deserve it." "They brought this problem on themselves." "What difference could I make anyway? That problem will never go away."

Imagine

At the other extreme from the stereotypes is what we call the "imagine," where you imagine how life would be for all of our society if the mission of your organization were fulfilled. You will definitely want to have some "outsiders" there to help you with this part. If you are a staff member, it is best to assume that you have become resigned and jaded about this. The fresh and idealistic perspective of regular folks out there in the world will be a welcome addition to this process.

What if that intractable problem you are working on were eradicated, or at least became preventable? What if no more youth were homeless? What if Internet access was available in every school? What if your researchers found the cure for that disease we most dread?

The "imagine" calls forth our expansive, generous, noble selves. It says: "That's not right." "That's not okay with me." "It shouldn't be that way." "They don't deserve that." "It's not fair." It leaves us indignant, saying, "We've got to do something about this!"

For the "street youth," some of the "imagines" might be: "Imagine if every child were wanted." "Imagine if parents weren't abusing children." "Imagine if people understood why some youth see life on the street as better than life at home." "Imagine a society where people understood and cared about children and were capable of raising them in a loving home."

Tell Them Straight

Given all the stereotypes and misconceptions about your work, if there were one thing you could tell the world about your organization's work or the people you serve, what would it be? If, for one moment, you could look them straight in the eye and tell them the one thing you have never been able to say before, what would you say?

It may be, "It's the least you can do," or "You don't even have a clue," or "Pay now or pay later," or "They are smarter than you think." It can even be, "We have a plan for fixing this problem."

What most groups discover in creating this straightforward statement is the extent to which they have been holding back in conveying the real emotion of their work. This is what your donors are hungry for.

YOUR ORGANIZATION'S ESSENTIAL STORY

To begin pulling this all together as something usable at your Point of Entry Events, think again about your organization's Essential Story. This is the one generic, almost archetypal story that, when told by anyone, always evokes emotion about your work. It may be a true story about one particular person or group or it may be a composite of several stories of people who have benefited from your work.

People will remember a story. Long after the specific facts have slipped from their minds, that story will linger.

I like to think of the Essential Story as the central core of the Emotional Hook. That is because, in telling it, it evokes every aspect of the Emotional Hook and calls people to action. Without insulting or demeaning any of your guests or donors, it calls forth those basic human emotions, cherished cultural values, deeply held stereotypes, hopes and dreams. It is a politically correct way to convey that one message you would like to convey if you could look them in the eye and wake them up to the real needs of your population. And, in telling the Essential Story, your rallying cry comes through without necessarily ever having to be said out loud.

THE ESSENTIAL STORY

After people have heard this story, they feel compelled to take action. They can no longer sit by complacently and allow this problem or need to exist without doing something about it.

Examples of the Essential Story might be the "homeless mother" story, the "pregnant teenager" story, the "rain forest destruction" story, or the "house-fire survivor" story.

Brainstorm with your staff and volunteers to see which stories are contenders, and then practice telling them. Do they move you? Do the stories evoke each element of the Emotional Hook? Would any one story alone compel someone to take action?

CONVEYING THE EMOTIONAL HOOK AT YOUR POINT OF ENTRY

Once you know the elements of the Emotional Hook and the Essential Story for your organization, you will want to integrate each of them throughout your Point of Entry Events using all the tools available to you. These become the ingredients that must be conveyed in your Visionary Leader Talk, your video, live or taped testimonials, letters, photos or tour. Take the time to think through specifically what you can do or say to evoke each of the five ingredients of the Emotional Hook pie at your Point of Entry Events. Make sure you touch on them all.

Furthermore, the Emotional Hook needs to naturally complement the Facts about your work—the statistics and the most basic questions we need to have answered. Each Fact should trigger the Emotional Hook. Every issue of your newsletter, every invitation, every phone call, mailing or e-mail, should contain some vestige of the Emotional Hook. Donors are counting on you to remind them of the Emotional Hook every time they come in contact with you. You and your organization are their reminder system for this critical issue. Do not back off.

Always, the message you are trying to convey is, "This work changes lives." No matter how abstract, how far removed from the day-to-day lives of the people who will ultimately benefit, you wouldn't be doing this work if you didn't believe it would, sooner or later, improve life for regular people. You must keep saying that. Boil it all down to the life of one family, one child, one villager. That is the only way people can get their hands around your issue. Make it human scale. Tell us how life will be better. Give us specific examples that trigger various elements of the Emotional Hook.

Using the Emotional Hook Responsibly

The Emotional Hook is a legitimate and powerful tool at your disposal. You have to be responsible about how you use your organization's Emotional Hook, walking the fine line between overdoing it and not stressing it enough. People will have emotional reactions to your work whether or not you plan for them to have those reactions. Once you know what those Emotional Hooks are, manage them responsibly. Use them to steer people in the direction of taking action.

Too much of an Emotional Hook can leave people feeling manipulated and embarrassed, even angry. You don't want them to direct their anger towards you! You want them to be stirred up about your issue, so they will want to support you in dealing effectively with the problem. Sometimes subtlety is better. Allude to the Emotional Hook, know that you have made your point and then leave it alone.

Resist any temptation to present your organization as the meek and struggling nonprofit trying to do good work, fighting the good fight. You have to be responsible for how important your work is, for what a difference it is making and will continue to make. You have to be genuinely moved by the work and unafraid to convey that. You have to believe and let your donors know you believe.

Ultimately, if you don't reach in and hook their hearts, they won't remember you for long. Rather than becoming their personal cause, you will be just one more needy cause in the world. The Emotional Hook helps people to discover for themselves that your organization is worthy of their fullest contribution. That is what you are after.

CHAPTER 6

CAPTURING NAMES
WITH PERMISSION

The third essential ingredient at a Point of Entry is that you must Capture the Name of each guest with their permission. What do we mean by permission? As I said earlier, one of the key distinguishing factors about the Raising More Money Model is that it is permission-based. We can only proceed around the circle with each donor or potential donor if we have that donor's permission.

In the old fundraising reality, we didn't care about permission— we just boldly blurted out our organization's story and asked people to give money. We were interrupting whatever they were doing to shift the conversation rapidly to our needs. Even if people responded "properly" with a check, they generally resented this approach and, left on their own, would probably not give again.

New-reality fundraising follows the same solid relationship-building principles dubbed "permission marketing" by technology marketing guru Seth Godin. His seminal work, *Permission Marketing*, says we must earn people's permission to market to them, one step at a time. Permission correlates with trust. To the extent that we trust someone, we give them more permission. Conversely, to the extent that we stop trusting them, we take away our permission. Godin defines four levels of permission, each of which must be earned incrementally. The ultimate level that we are aiming for is what he calls "intravenous permission."

Most nonprofit organizations have at least a small number of "intravenous" donors. This does not mean that these donors will say yes to every dollar you ask them for. It means that you have enough permission with them to ask for their advice and support, to let your hair down a bit and treat them as insiders of your organization's family. It means that you do not need to have your story sugarcoated and wrapped up in a pretty package with a big red bow before you can talk to them. For these donors, your organization is not merely a passing fancy. It is their true work. As such, they welcome your calls and visits. They want to hear from you. And, generally speaking, they want to give to you.

THE SIGN-IN CARD

I recommend you print up simple sign-in cards that each guest fills out personally at the sign-in table. This makes follow-up simpler than a guest book or other sign-in sheet.

SAMPLE: **SIGN-IN CARD**

Name(s)

Address

City   State   Zip

Day Phone   Evening Phone

E-Mail
Guest of
Date:

(Free Arts of Arizona, Phoenix, AZ)

YOU MUST CAPTURE THE NAMES

Capturing names with permission often becomes the deciding variable in whether or not the event you have worked so hard to produce is actually a Point of Entry. Think of the many speaking opportunities your Visionary Leader and other staff members have to tell your story to the community. There are all the community meetings, civic groups, faith groups—the whole speaker's circuit that someone in your organization may have worked hard to create.

Most of those events do not qualify as Points of Entry. Even if your speaker gives people the facts and the Emotional Hook, if you have not captured the names of the guests with their permission, they will not have attended a true Point of Entry. You will not have secured their permission—either explicit or implicit—to follow up with them after the presentation.

Do not stop speaking at these events. They are wonderful marketing opportunities for your organization. However, do not delude yourself by thinking that anything further will necessarily ever come of your contact with the people in the audience—except, of course, for those few people who are so interested in your work that they come up to talk with you after the presentation. With those people, you may ask naturally for their business card, ask if they would like you to stay in touch with them, or invite them to your Point of Entry.

Once you become focused on the importance of capturing people's names with their permission, you may find other ways to do this legitimately. We will cover this further in Chapter 15 on Point of Entry Conversion Events.

CHAPTER 7

CREATING A TREASURE MAP

As you begin to see the merit of Point of Entry Events, you will naturally wonder who to invite to them. Given the personal nature of this model, it only makes sense to start with the people who already are connected to you in some way. You can branch out from there, following the stream of passion and natural word-of-mouth connections that link people. Before you know it, the whole system will snowball.

Rather than spending time trying to interest the obvious wealthy donors in your community who may not know or care about your organization, take the time to brainstorm about the natural supporters who are lurking right under your nose. We use the term "Treasure Map" because it identifies the natural treasure around you right now. You don't have to go out of your way to find these people. You don't have to make your selections based on wealth or social status. Include everyone and brainstorm away.

LEARNING TO DRAW A TREASURE MAP

This brainstorming exercise is best done with a team of people—ideally, the same team that will be involved in implementing the model over the next year or two. The more diverse your team members, the more diverse the Treasure Map. At some point, you will want to do this exercise with your board as well. If you are the person who will be leading the group through the process, be sure to practice it first with a small group of staff members, family or friends.

Get out a large piece of paper and colored markers and lead your team through the process. Begin by drawing a circle in the center of the page. Put the name of your organization in the circle.

Then surround your organization, like the spokes on a wheel, with all the other groups you come in contact with on a regular basis. Start with groups like your board, staff, volunteers, donors and funders, vendors and other groups in the community that you interact with regularly.

TREASURE MAP
GROUPS AND ORGANIZATIONS

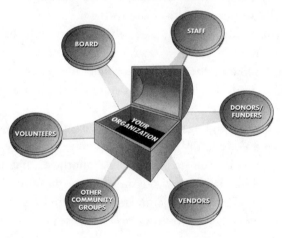

You may be able to subdivide groups like your board or staff further into former board, former board presidents, founding board members and so on. Similarly, your volunteers may be subdivided by the type of projects they are involved with. United Way, for example, has many substrata of loaned executive volunteers—depending on the industry they came from or the industry they will be soliciting. Red Cross volunteers may be subcategorized as blood volunteers, disaster volunteers, health and safety volunteers, and so on.

Take the time to brainstorm as many groups as you can think of. You can lump all the civic groups under one category. All the other community organizations you interact with may be a group or you may choose to subdivide them into categories like law enforcement, schools, other arts organizations, etc.

The more detail you can put into the Treasure Map as you list these groups, the more you will be able to target their specific resources and self-interests in the later steps of the Treasure Map process.

RESOURCES IN ABUNDANCE

Now, with a differently colored pen or marker, list the resources which each of these groups has in abundance. Why? Because this is an abundance-based model of fundraising. It presumes people will naturally want to give that which they have plenty of.

Most of us do not like saying no; it makes us feel mean and uncaring. People would rather say yes when you ask them. It is much easier for them to say yes if you are asking them to give you something you know they already have in excess. For some people you may not know what that is, but it usually doesn't take long to find out when you think about who you could ask.

Go back to the Treasure Map and start listing out the abundant resources of your board, staff, volunteers, etc. Take the time to look closely at each group or subgroup. You will notice that their resources may be different. For example, your board in general might have an abundance of passion, commitment, expertise, contacts and money. Yet your former board presidents may have additional resources, such as a long-term commitment to your organization, or certain connections in the community.

Your volunteers might have an abundance of time, expertise, connections and money as well. When you categorize volunteers by the type of program they are involved with, you will see more resources. Literacy tutors, for example, may have an abundance of teaching skill or an abundance of contacts in the educational field or an abundance of passion and personal stories to share from the people they have tutored.

How about your staff? They have an abundance of passion, firsthand stories about the good work of your organization, time (because they are being paid for their time at work) and expertise. Staff in different programs and departments will have different stories and different connections. Hospice nurses will have had direct contact with family members. Department directors may have more contact with the doctors. Take the time to do this with each group. What resources do they have in abundance?

TREASURE MAP
ABUNDANT RESOURCES

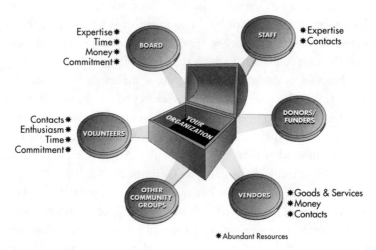

SELF-INTEREST

Next, go back over each group and ask what their self-interest would be in coming to your Point of Entry Event. What is the value or benefit for them in attending?

Let's pause a minute to talk about self-interest. Self-interest is a good thing. It drives everything we do. For example, you have a definite self-interest in reading this book. Maybe that self-interest is finding new ideas, maybe it is pleasing the boss, or maybe it is because you wanted a break from your work. Self-interest is always there, and as a person who is interested in raising funds, you should think of it as a very useful resource.

Self-interest can range from the most negative and selfish motives all the way to the most noble and inspiring. Consider the full range of self-interest as you go back to your Treasure Map and list the self-interests of each group.

Consider, for example, your donors or funders. What benefit does being connected to you have for them? Ask yourself, "What is in this for them?" Yes, they may want a tax write-off, but this is rarely the sole reason for making a gift. For most donors, a major self-interest is feeling good about making the gift and feeling they are making a difference. For some donors, self-interest is paying back someone for something they once received. Or maybe they have a personal connection to the services you offer. Or they feel that giving to your organization is a kind of insurance, that what you are committed to preventing won't happen to them. Guilt can be a self-interest, as well as impressing others and looking good. Maybe they are giving because they think it will help their child or grandchild to be accepted into your private school or college.

Look at the self-interest of your volunteers. Why are they involved with you? Perhaps it is to make a difference, to contribute their talents, to learn new skills, to build their resume for their next job, to give back, to feel important, to keep busy, and on and on. What about your board? For some, their self-interest is to please a boss who "asked" them to serve on your board. For others, it is a personal connection, a way of giving back, or a feel-good thing.

Donor for donor, self-interest is a key driver of your self-sustaining individual giving program. The sooner you know your donors' self-interest, whatever it may be, the easier it will be to customize your fundraising program to their needs. Down the road, as they become lifelong donors, you will want to think back to the self-interest that led to their involvement in the first place.

TREASURE MAP
SELF INTERESTS

Expertise ✴
Time ✴
Money ✴
Commitment ✴
Make a Difference ✪
Feel Good ✪
Personal Connection ✪
Please the Boss ✪

BOARD

STAFF

✴Expertise
✴Contacts
✪Paycheck
✪Make a Difference

Contacts ✴
Enthusiasm ✴
Time ✴
Commitment ✴
Make a Difference ✪
Contribute Talents ✪
Learn New Skills ✪
Socialize ✪

VOLUNTEERS

YOUR ORGANIZATION

DONORS/ FUNDERS

✴Money
✴Time
✴Contacts
✪Tax Write-off
✪Feel Good
✪Make a Difference

OTHER COMMUNITY GROUPS

VENDORS

✴Goods & Services
✴Money
✴Contacts
✪Look Good to Others
✪They Really Care
✪New Business Contacts

✴Abundant Resources
✪Self-Interests

FANTASY GROUPS

Next, looking back at your Treasure Map, add in some fantasy categories. Who is not yet on your map that you would love to have be associated with your organization? Whose involvement would leverage a whole world of support and credibility? Add those people to your Treasure Map, too. Some typical fantasy categories include celebrities, athletes, corporate executives and media figures. For some organizations, having the support of a local opinion leader, a religious leader or an expert on your issue could quickly leverage your story into the larger community.

Let yourself play with this one. This is why it is fun to do a Treasure Map with a group of people.

TREASURE MAP
FANTASY GROUP

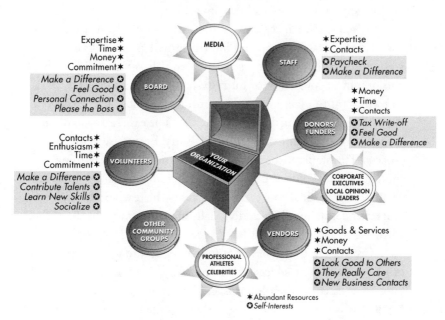

CONNECTING THE GROUPS

Finally, draw connecting lines between those groups on your Treasure Map who already talk to each other. You will see instantly how fast news travels. If a handful of people come to your sizzling Point of Entry Event, who else will they tell?

If your staff talks to your volunteers, draw a connecting line between those two groups. If your board and vendors talk only occasionally, you might draw a dotted line. For those groups who don't talk to each other at all, draw no connecting lines. Be sure to include your fantasy groups. Who on your organization's Treasure Map already might be talking with them? It is worth taking the time to go through this one category at a time. It can spark many insights.

Before moving on, stand back from your Treasure Map and notice which groups have the most lines connecting them to other groups. There may be so many lines leading to or from that group that it looks like a traffic jam. What does that tell you? These groups are key to leveraging others. They could naturally invite the people in these other groups to attend your Point of Entry Events because they are speaking to them all the time anyway.

A frequent example of a traffic-jam group is your staff. The staff is likely to be one group on the Treasure Map that talks to nearly every other group. What does that tell you? It should tell you that staff buy-in to your Point of Entry system is critical to your success. You will want to make a special effort to involve staff in the process. We will explore this further in Chapter 20. The easiest way to do this is to have special staff-only Point of Entry Events early on in the process. The staff can be invaluable in critiquing and refining the content at your Point of Entry. I remember how much we modified what we said at our school tours after taking the teachers through the tours and debriefing them individually about how to talk about the curriculum.

Conversely, if they have not fully bought into the process, staff can be your biggest adversary. Go out of your way to let the staff know how essential their input is and how much you will need their support as you begin having regularly scheduled Points of Entry.

PERSONAL TREASURE MAP

Next, give each team member a blank piece of paper and have them make a personal Treasure Map for themselves. Start by having people put their own names in the middle. Then have them go through the same steps of adding the groups they naturally come in contact with, what each group has in abundance, the self-interests of the groups in coming to a Point of Entry Event for your organization, their fantasy groups, and the lines connecting those who know each other. Give them enough time to get into doing the exercise. They probably will be surprised by all the treasure they have. Give them the time to go through all the steps.

Now, assuming your team has already attended a Point of Entry Event and knows what you are talking about, you can ask them to look back to their personal Treasure Maps and make a list of ten to twenty individuals they would feel comfortable inviting to a Point of

TREASURE MAP
WHO TALKS TO WHOM?

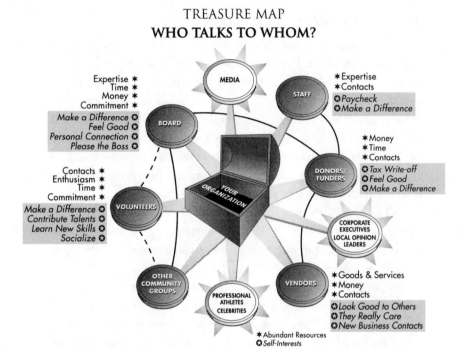

Expertise *
Time *
Money *
Commitment *
Make a Difference ✪
Feel Good ✪
Personal Connection ✪
Please the Boss ✪

*Expertise
*Contacts
✪ *Paycheck*
✪ *Make a Difference*

*Money
*Time
*Contacts
✪ *Tax Write-off*
✪ *Feel Good*
✪ *Make a Difference*

Contacts *
Enthusiasm *
Time *
Commitment *
Make a Difference ✪
Contribute Talents ✪
Learn New Skills ✪
Socialize ✪

MEDIA

STAFF

BOARD

DONORS/
FUNDERS

VOLUNTEERS

YOUR
ORGANIZATION

CORPORATE
EXECUTIVES
LOCAL OPINION
LEADERS

OTHER
COMMUNITY
GROUPS

PROFESSIONAL
ATHLETES
CELEBRITIES

VENDORS

*Goods & Services
*Money
*Contacts
✪ *Look Good to Others*
✪ *They Really Care*
✪ *New Business Contacts*

*Abundant Resources
✪ *Self-Interests*

Entry. Encourage them to have their list include people from each group on their Treasure Map, not just the "safest" groups of friends and family. Once they see the self-interest people have in coming to a Point of Entry, inviting them will become more of a game than a chore. They will realize that the person at the health club had already mentioned their interest in the environment or their mother's health problem. In other words, these people might actually *want* to come to learn more about your organization.

Some people on your team will have long, long lists of people they could invite. Do not make them feel awkward or embarrassed. There will naturally be people with more contacts than others. Long-time volunteers may have extensive lists of former volunteers they would like to invite. People in the health care profession may have more people on their personal Treasure Maps with self-interest in your health care work. Give everyone the time to make their lists or tell them to finish them after the meeting.

TREASURE MAP INTERVIEWS

Encourage your team to conduct formal or informal Treasure Map Interviews. The Treasure Map Interview is a powerful tool for deepening the dialog with prior and potential donors in an open-ended, nonthreatening way. The sequencing of the questions provides a natural lead-in to inviting people to attend a Point of Entry. If you take the time to really listen, people will tell you everything you need to know about precisely how they would like to be involved. In fact, you may notice people talking themselves into becoming more involved with you, just in the process of the interview.

The biggest challenge with Treasure Map Interviews is remembering that you are not trying to get anyone to give you anything, including money. Your only objective is to listen carefully to the other person's responses.

You do not need to schedule a formal interview time to conduct a Treasure Map Interview, unless you prefer to do so. You can work these questions into your normal conversations with people. Remember, if the people you will be interviewing are on your Treasure Map, they are people you see or talk to from time to time anyway.

It is fine to ask them the interview questions while you are driving somewhere together, having lunch or attending a meeting. We often recommend workshop participants start by interviewing someone close to them who is "easy," such as a spouse or partner, child or parent, neighbor or close friend. Often, the people closest to us have plenty of thoughts and opinions about our organizations; we just never think to ask them. Another easy first interview can be done with a stranger on a bus or airplane.

Here are the suggested Treasure Map Interview questions to get you going. You do not need to use them all. Once you get the hang of this, you will be able to modify and tailor them to your own style and situation. You may select different questions for different people you interview.

Treasure Map Interview Questions

1. *What do you know about our organization?*

2. *What images come to mind when you think of us?*
   You may be surprised to learn that, even if they have never heard of your organization before, there will be certain images that come to mind anyway.

3. *How did you come to know about us or become involved with us?*
   Let them take as long as they like to tell you their story.

4. *What do you like about being a friend of our organization?*
   You may be pleasantly surprised by all the nice things people have to say. Note which things matter most to them.

5. *Where or how do you think we are really missing the boat?*
   Notice your tendency to become defensive here. Put yourself in their shoes. These may be things they have been harboring for a while—things they really do want to communicate. If they sense that you are trying to justify or make excuses in any way, they will back off. You will not have gathered the critical feedback you are seeking. Resist the temptation to talk at all. Just be quiet and listen.

6. *What advice do you have for us?*
   Regardless of how well they know you, they will have advice for you. Everyone loves giving advice.

7. *What cues might we have missed from you?*
   You might hear things like: "After all the years I've been sending in those $100 checks, I'm surprised no one called to ask me to give more."

8. *How could we tell our story better?*
   People often say things like: "I wish you'd stop sending me those long boring newsletters. I only like the part with the stories about the people you've helped."

9.   *What could we do to involve more people?*
      This is where people often suggest names of others you should
      call. Or they may offer to connect you with the person arrang-
      ing speakers for a particular business group. If you have done a
      good job of listening up until now, the person will definitely be
      forthcoming with suggestions.

      Remember, the Treasure Map Interviews have no hidden agenda.
You are not trying to get anyone to give you anything. Your only
objective is to listen carefully to the other person's responses.
      At the end of the interview, be sure to thank them sincerely for
their time. Jot down what they actually said, not your thoughts and
opinions about what they said. Also write down any next steps that
may be needed based on the input you received. Be sure these notes
are kept in your database, which should have a "notes" section for
each person you interview.

CHAPTER 8

INVITING PEOPLE TO POINTS OF ENTRY

Now that you have your staff, your board and your team ready to go, how are you going to ensure that they convey a consistent message at the point each guest is invited to attend the Point of Entry?

Most invitations to your regularly scheduled Points of Entry in a Box will be extended word-of-mouth. There will be no need for fancy invitations, sorting by zip code, postage, etc. These events will become part of the informal culture of your organization. That does not mean, however, that you won't need to nudge the process along a bit.

The first way to do that is by offering a suggested script to all of the people who will be inviting others. You can print this up on a little card and go over it in person with each inviter. Here is a suggested script for inviting people to Points of Entry:

**SAMPLE WORDING FOR INVITING GUESTS
TO A POINT OF ENTRY**

Hello, Mary. You know how excited I am about the _____ organization. I've been involved with them now for some time and I really feel they are changing the way people feel about _____. They've got a very unique approach and a great new program for _____. They are trying to get the word out into the community about their

work and to get feedback about their programs and services. I know you have talked with me before about your interest in solving this problem right here in our community.

The organization has begun offering a one-hour program and tour for people to see their work firsthand. I'd love to have you come and meet the real visionary who is the director and some of the great staff. You won't be asked to make any financial contribution, but we would welcome your advice and feedback. The next dates and times of our tours are _____.

Notice that the emphasis is on your organization's need to spread the word in the community and to gather feedback about how you are perceived. After all, that is the main purpose of the Point of Entry.

In terms of who to invite first, encourage everyone on your team to invite the "easy" people on their list first, such as the people from their personal Treasure Maps who clearly have a strong self-interest in learning more about the program. That way you will have some early, significant successes as you are refining and testing your Point of Entry content. And these passionate early guests will be eager to give you honest feedback and to invite others.

Once a guest agrees to attend, the inviter needs to call the person in charge of putting on the Points of Entry within the organization to confirm. This process will help with your planning and also let your inviters know that you have a system for anticipating and taking care of their guests.

When the date is more than a week away, the inviter will need to follow up by phone or e-mail to reconfirm the guest's attendance. This call can make all the difference, even for guests who truly want to come to the event. People get busy and other things intervene. When they wake up on the morning they said they would come to your Point of Entry Event, it may not look like their top priority. A call the day before from the person who invited them will further ensure that the guest will actually show up. Ideally, their inviter will be attending the event as well, and has already offered to pick them up and take them—two additional incentives to attend.

Be sure to close the loop with the inviter if they are not able to attend with their guest. After the Point of Entry, call and let them know how excited their friend was and encourage them to call or send a note to thank the person for coming. This thank-you from the inviter does not in any way substitute for the official Follow-Up Call made within one week by the designated staff person or volunteer in charge of all follow-up. That person follows the specified script to gather data about the guest's level and area of interest. In other words, the inviter has no further obligation to shepherd the guest around the Raising More Money cycle, unless they choose to be involved as part of the organization's Raising More Money implementation team. The sooner the guest is weaned away from their friend the inviter and becomes bonded to the mission and work of the organization, the better.

Finally, as mentioned earlier, give the inviters the kudos and recognition they deserve in front of their fellow board members, team members or volunteers. If their first experience of inviting someone to a Point of Entry is a positive one, they will be predisposed to doing it again.

Remember too that the way you take care of the inviters tells them how you will take care of their guests—namely with the same sincere interest and consideration as you would give any potential lifelong donor.

CHAPTER 9

DESIGNING A
KNOW-THY-DONOR PROGRAM

O ne of the first questions I ask when I start working with an organization is the obvious: "How many active donors do you have?" Often they proudly tell me a very large number, somewhere in the many thousands. Next question: "How many of those donors does someone here actually know?" This means someone has, at a minimum, talked to them in person or on the phone. Invariably, the answer to this question is: "Not many."

From time to time, we are called by progressive, new-reality, direct-mail companies to ask if we will work with their clients. They have done an excellent job of attracting new donors and increasing their gifts over the years. "We've reached the limit of what we can do for these organizations with direct mail. They've got to get to know these donors personally and grow them into major donors."

They are right. Most organizations do not need new donors. They have plenty of existing donors. Rather than ramping up to start a massive program for inviting brand new people to Points of Entry in hopes of cultivating them to become donors, it is a far wiser investment to get to know their existing donors.

The system outlined in this chapter could also be called a strategy for getting to know your long lists of nearly anonymous direct-mail, telemarketing or online donors. Also, if your organization has a large number of members that no one really knows personally, this system is ideal for beginning the process of converting those members to donors.

This is called a Know-Thy-Donor Program. It provides a personalized, customized approach for converting people from mere names and zip codes on a piece of paper to real people with faces and voices who can come to live Point of Entry Events and become part of your organization's family of lifelong donors.

Think of yourself as one of those loyal donors to your favorite organization. You have been giving faithfully for years, sending in checks in response to mail, phone or online appeals annually, quarterly or monthly. Yet no one has ever called you to say thank you or to acknowledge your gift in person. It is a wonder you keep giving at all.

STRATIFY YOUR DONORS BY GIFT LEVEL

Start your Know-Thy-Donor Program by getting the real numbers about your organization. How many individual donors have given to you in the last two years? What is each donor's total gift for each of those years? You may be surprised to see how those $25-a-month checks add up, all from one loyal donor.

Now, classify the donors you have. How many give you, annually:

- $1,000 and above?
- $500 - $999?
- $250 - $499?
- $100 - $249?

Don't be surprised to find some who give more than $10,000 a year without a personal contact from you.

What are they telling you with this gift? For whatever reason, they are believers in your work. They may have only a superficial understanding of the work of your organization, yet they give. Perhaps they had a family member with the disease you are working to eradicate. Maybe their mother or father received services from your organization many years ago.

If you are working to build a self-sustaining individual giving program that is based on one-on-one personal relationships, knowing more about each donor would be a great help. And there is only one way to find out—ask them!

A HIGH-LEVEL THANKATHON

Once you have analyzed the stratification of your existing donors, choose the cutoff level for your first round of calls. Let's say you decide to call all donors who give $500 or more a year and that you have one hundred of them.

Start your Know-Thy-Donor Program by enlisting the support of three to five of your best and most passionate people. They should also be people who like talking on the telephone. It may be a mixed group of board, staff and volunteers.

Before you give them the list of donors to be called and a recommended script, it is wise for the most senior development staff person or volunteer to make five or ten of these calls personally. That way you will get consistent feedback, all screened through the eyes and ears of the same caller. Based on what you learn in the first ten calls, you can then design a broader telephone survey that can be used by your team of callers.

How should you start the calls? Yes, with a gracious and humble thank-you. The main purpose of the call is to thank and appreciate the donor for their loyal support (and their recent gift, if your timing is right). If you accomplish nothing else on this call, be sure they know how much you appreciate them.

SUGGESTED SCRIPT FOR THE THANKATHON CALL

Hello, Ms. _____. My name is _____. I'm on the board of _____. You've been a loyal supporter for several/many years and we're calling to thank you. (Pause for response.) We're doing a little survey to learn what we could be doing better. Would you have a few minutes now for me to ask for your thoughts and advice?

TREASURE MAP INTERVIEW QUESTIONS

Then, slowly, ask three or four of the open-ended Treasure Map Interview questions, as listed on page 85, noting the donor's answers along the way. At a minimum, I recommend you ask the following questions:

1. How did you come to know about us or become involved with us?

2. What advice do you have for us?

3. How better could we be telling our story?

KNOW-THY-DONOR PROGRAM

① STRATIFY
② HIGH LEVEL THANKATHON
③ INTERVIEW
④ INVITE

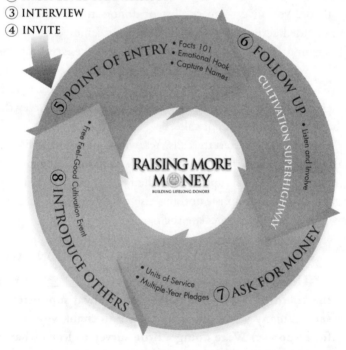

INVITE THEM TO A POINT OF ENTRY

Each call should end with an invitation to attend a Point of Entry or Point of Re-Entry Event, and to bring others if they would like. If they agree to attend, follow up with a confirmation card and a reconfirmation call the day before. Offer to provide transportation if necessary.

Your calling team can do the phoning in a group one afternoon or evening, or they can make their calls on their own from their home or workplace. Be sure they turn in their notes. Imagine, for example, a team of five callers with each caller reaching five people a week. If you debrief well, you will have enough feedback to customize the next phase of the program.

I have seen board members get so excited about this that they recommend a Donor Services Representative Program or buddy system for pairing a volunteer or staff member with each donor above a certain dollar amount to be the primary person to stay in contact with this donor. Imagine being a donor who hears from someone at their favorite charitable organization three or four times a year—including invitations to a variety of special Free Feel-Good Cultivation Events. When it is time for making their annual gift next year, they will be hard-pressed to say no to a request for a larger gift. They may even feel connected enough to become a member of your Multiple-Year Giving Society when asked, especially if their pledge will be doubled by a matching gift Challenge Fund.

Remember, these are your cherished donors, those names on your mailing list who are sending in small and medium-sized gifts on a regular basis. Show them the respect and care you would show your greatest treasures. And then show them the great work of your organization!

FOLLOW-UP: KEEP THEM ON THE CYCLE

Next, get these prior donors officially on your cycle. Dazzle them with your Point of Entry: the Facts, the Emotional Hook, the needs, all the trimmings. Follow up within a week and get their feedback. How else might they like to become involved? Who else would they recommend you invite to a similar event? Then deliver on what they are requesting. Follow through impeccably with feedback on all their suggestions. Thank them for sending their friend to the next introductory event. Find lots of reasons to have more contact with them. Keep thinking of what else you might do to be responsive to their unique concerns.

Keep this system going. Have your phoning team keep calling and interviewing more prior donors from your database, moving down to the $100 to $499 donors, and so on. Keep inviting donors to Point of Entry Events. Keep reeducating, reinspiring and thanking them, the more personally the better.

One caution: You will come across donors who have been giving in response to mail and telephone solicitations who do not want more personal contact with you. They prefer an arms-length relationship. One option is to offer to have a One-on-One Point of Entry Event for them, which we will discuss more in Chapter 10. You can send them a copy of your video and follow up by phone a week later. Or you can keep them on your personal phoning list to update them as often as they would like to hear about your new programs and your needs.

Remember, this is a personalized, one-on-one model. People have their own distinct preferences. The thing that will impress them most is if you listen to how they are telling you they want to be kept in contact with and then follow through by doing exactly what they ask. Conversely, the thing that will annoy them most is if, after asking their opinion, you don't follow their advice when dealing with them.

Stay focused on this Know-Thy-Donor Program and you will see your contributions increase. You will be cultivating your base of lifelong donors.

SPECIAL CONCERNS OF
MEMBERSHIP ORGANIZATIONS

Membership organizations have one distinct hurdle to over-come in fundraising. Members often pay with the primary objective of receiving specific membership benefits. As such, most members do not think of themselves as donors. They think of themselves as members. This is often the case with members of arts organizations, for example, who join to receive preferred seating, parking privileges, magazine subscriptions, early notification of events and other specific benefits. Yet when asked to give, the initial response of most members is that they are already "giving" to the organization.

In other words, you have permission from these members to treat them only as members—until you request more permission from them. For members, that is the purpose of the Know-Thy-Donor (in this case, we could say Know-Thy-Member) Program—it allows you to connect with members to see if they are willing to give you permission to start courting them as donors. In other words, would they even consider coming to a Point of Entry or Point of Entry Conversion Event? In most cases, if executed with discretion, the answer will be yes.

Think of an organization you "belong" to—a museum, a theater, or perhaps an organization like the National Geographic Society. I belonged to that organization for years, but mainly because that was the only way to get their wonderful magazine. Eventually, I accumulated enough stacks of magazines—which were so beautiful and educational that I refused to throw them away—that it became time to "terminate my membership."

Imagine if someone had contacted me in person at some point in all of those years. Imagine that another member like me had called me and said, "Gee, I was just like you a few years ago, enjoying those great magazines and thinking that was all the National Geographic Society was about. Then someone called me and told me about the incredible work they are doing all over the world. The magazine is just the tip of the iceberg. Once I learned more, I found there was one project that particularly interested me. I learned that in addition to being a member, I could become a contributor to the larger work of the organization, just like I am with my university or religious organization."

Suddenly I'm invited into the fold. I'm educated in a sensitive way by someone like myself. She doesn't make me feel embarrassed for not knowing about the real work of the National Geographic Society, she just tells me more.

In fact, she ends by inviting me to a special evening being held in my city for loyal members like me who might want to learn more about the special projects underway by the larger Society. There is no charge to attend and no obligation to become more involved. "It's just something we offer to help people understand our work. Feel free to bring others who you think might be interested."

Who could say no to that?

Now, contrast that with a cold call over dinner from a paid caller asking if I'd like to renew my magazine subscription by renewing my membership. The difference is striking.

This is the kind of care that needs to be taken in implementing a Know-Thy-Donor program. As with each aspect of the model, it must be customized to your organization and tested over time to see what works. That is why I recommend having a small, high-level team of callers who can debrief frequently and tweak the plan as many times as necessary until you find what works best. From there, you can extend the program to more callers and more people called at different levels of gift or membership.

Even after you have designed a strategy for successfully converting your members to donors, do not put an end to your membership program. It is an enviable source of new potential people to come to your Point of Entry Events—people who already have a connection to your programs or services, just like I did with National Geographic.

CHAPTER 10

THE ONE-ON-ONE
POINT OF ENTRY

O nce you have customized the essential components of your organization's Point of Entry, you can begin to play with the components a bit. A simple adaptation, and one that will come in handy, is the One-on-One Point of Entry.

While the focus of your effort will be on systematizing the Points of Entry on a monthly or semi-monthly basis, there will be many occasions when your board members, volunteers and staff will find themselves naturally in a position to have a brief conversation with a friend or colleague about your organization. This is especially useful for busy executive directors and board members who are already interacting with high-level people in your community on other matters. By inserting a brief Point of Entry element into the course of their conversation, these same friends and colleagues will have been connected to your work and they may give you permission to stay in contact with them. Whether or not they choose to learn more, you will have spread the word and perhaps, in a Follow-Up Call, they will elect to come to a Point of Entry Event or to refer someone else who truly is passionate about your mission.

In the coaching that follows our workshops, we often hear remarkable stories from people who do the One-on-One Point of Entry with old friends or with strangers on airplanes or while waiting in a line at the bank. Once you have gotten your "routine" put together, it should take you no more than two minutes to educate and genuinely move someone to tears about the great work of your organization.

THE ONE-ON-ONE POINT OF ENTRY

1. **Who we are**. You have to tell them the name of your organization.

2. **Top three programs.** Even if you have fifteen or twenty programs, figure out which three you will focus on. Try to choose the "juiciest" programs that will relate to the following points.

3. **Three little-known facts about our work.** Here is where you insert the Top Three Facts from your standard Point of Entry in a Box. These are the facts that dispel their unspoken stereotypes and myths about your work. Make them interesting and easy to remember.

4. **Why I work here.** Here is where you tell your own story—the short version. Let them know this is much more than a job for you. If you lost a family member to the disease you are now working to cure, tell them that. People respect a personal connection. If you don't have such a connection, tell them what keeps you working there.

5. **"I'll never forget the story about ..."** This is where you tell the Essential Story—again, the short version. Practice telling it until you can do it in thirty seconds or less. It can be done.

6. **"Would you be interested in more information?"** or: "Would you like to come to our regularly scheduled Point of Entry?" If they are interested, ask for their business card and give them yours.

That's it. In less than two minutes you have conveyed the Facts and the Emotional Hook. Then be quiet and listen closely to the person's response. Even if they are not interested personally in the work of your organization, if you have moved them with the facts and the stories, they will have been touched enough to thank you and to suggest other people they know who you might want to contact. At best, they will jump right in and offer to help you or say that they want to learn more by coming to one of your regularly scheduled Point of Entry Events.

When you get back to your office, be sure this person's name gets added to your database and to your follow-up tracking system. If they said they would like to come to a Point of Entry, you need to be the one to call and personally invite them. Do not delegate this to anyone else. Remember, this personal connection is key to the success of the Raising More Money Model. Make it as easy as possible for them to say yes. You can even encourage them to bring a friend, if that would make them feel more comfortable.

If you train your team to do One-on-One Points of Entry, they will become your roving ambassadors in the community. Whenever they attend social events or business gatherings, they will be armed and ready to go. This is especially useful at the year-end holiday time when your ambassadors will be standing around punchbowls reconnecting with friends. They will now have a new answer to the question: What are you doing these days? We will talk more about this in Chapter 24, "Points of Entry and the Holiday Season."

CHAPTER 11

SAMPLE POINTS OF ENTRY

Now we can begin to synthesize the generic components into several sample Point of Entry Events for different types of organizations of different sizes. Please note that these are not intended to be generic templates for Point of Entry Events. Instead, consider them as sample components that you might pick and choose from as you customize your Point of Entry.

EXAMPLE 1

In-office Point of Entry Event for a medium-sized urban Red Cross chapter.

Design Concerns:

- While most people assume everyone knows what the Red Cross does out in the "field," many Red Cross chapters feel they have relatively little "action" to show people at an in-office Point of Entry.

- How to showcase other little-known Red Cross programs.

- Staff members are often out of office working on projects and not available to talk about their programs.

Solution:

Name of Point of Entry:

Getting to Know Your Red Cross

Setting:

Office conference room was re-tooled inexpensively as a mock Red Cross triage center like the kind used during a real disaster. Gripping photos on the walls with captions of quotes from the families who had been saved or helped by Red Cross.

Top Three Frequently Asked Questions:

- Why does the Red Cross need my money? I thought you were funded by the government.

- We don't have many "disasters" here in our area. What does the Red Cross do here anyway?

- What are the demographics of the people who receive your service? Must you be low-income to qualify?

Top Three Facts:

- We have ___ serious house fires in our community each month. That's ___ families a year who are displaced. Red Cross provides each of them with cash, a hotel or motel room and the supplies they need to setup temporary housing.

- Our community uses _____ pints of blood per month for vital medical needs right here. There is currently a shortage of _____ pints per month.

- In addition to connecting family members with their loved ones in the military, we connect Holocaust survivors to long-lost family members. In the last year alone, we made ___ such connections.

Essential Story:

Family saved after house fire. Quote from little girl and mother.

Format:

1. **CAPTURE NAMES:** Sign-in table with individual sign-in cards in the hall outside the conference room. People sign in as they enter

2. **WELCOME:** Board Member

3. **VISIONARY LEADER TALK:** Executive Director

    a. Why I work here

    b. What I used to think the Red Cross did, and what I know now

    c. Here's what we're not able to do enough of, and why we need private support

4. **EMOTIONAL HOOK:** How the Essential Story and other stories will be told

    a. Seven-minute video (three minutes from a national Red Cross video and four minutes from a local TV news story about this Red Cross chapter)

    b. Live testimonial from a fire survivor and from a Red Cross disaster volunteer

    c. Demonstration of how the triage unit works during a real disaster

    d. Tour of the remainder of the offices, stopping at the desks of two staff members who work on nondisaster programs (Refugee Resettlement program and Holocaust Survivors program)

EXAMPLE 2

In-office Point of Entry for urban child abuse program.

Design Concerns:

- Subject matter is highly confidential; there is nothing to show people firsthand.
- No client testimonials.
- Staff works offsite—in courtrooms, hospitals and schools.

Solution:

Name of Point of Entry:

If These Walls Could Talk

Setting:

Office conference room and tour

Top Three FAQs:

- What are the demographics of child abusers? Age, income, ethnicity?
- Why can't we just lock these bad people up? Why does this problem persist?
- Is there any way to end this problem? It seems so hopeless.

Top Three Facts:

- Children who have been abused are ___ times more likely to become adults with other problems, such as learning disabilities, substance abuse, incarceration. They are ___% more likely to abuse their own children.
- Early intervention works to reverse this cycle—services such as counseling, medical support, advocacy through the court system, placement in a permanent home. These are the very services we offer.

- In our community, we have ___ cases of child abuse reported weekly. We are only able to serve ___ of those cases. Someone here has to tell the others that we are unable to serve them. There is no other organization that provides the same counseling and advocacy services we do.

Essential Story:

Staff member accompanying child to hospital exam after abuse incident; later telling about happy adoption placement and high school graduation story.

Format:

1. **CAPTURE NAMES:** Sign-in table at entrance

2. **WELCOME:** Volunteer or Board Member

3. **VISIONARY LEADER TALK:** Executive Director

   a. This problem exists right here in our community

   b. We've been around for ___ years and have placed hundreds of children in permanent homes

   c. We still turn away ___ children per week. We know how to help these children; we just don't have the resources

   d. My dream for this organization and this community is…

4. **EMOTIONAL HOOK:** How the Essential Story and other stories will be told

   a. Photos of happy kids around the office—kids running and playing, studying, being kids

   b. Live testimonial from volunteer or staff

   c. Tour of office:

      i. In each staff member's cubicle, have photos of children and an audiotape player.

ii. Tour leader says, "The staff member in this office works with children as they are first referred to the program. Here is a tape of one staff member telling us the story of a little boy she worked with recently."

iii. Next office of the staff member who works with the court system to find safe placement for the children. Audiotape of him describing a typical day or typical case situation.

iv. Last office: the counselor's office, decorated with kid stuff and toys. Audio of the counselor reading a letter of thanks from a prior client now in college.

EXAMPLE 3

Point of Entry on the road for a national rainforest protection membership organization. (This same format will work for an international relief organization or a grassroots membership organization.)

Design Concerns:

- Members are geographically dispersed.
- The work of the organization is abstract with only a few actual projects underway. All project sites are located in other countries.
- Members are accustomed to being passive; they do not think of themselves as "donors." They became members because they wanted certain benefits (magazine subscription, briefings on cutting-edge environmental issues).

Solution:

Name of Point of Entry:

Member Briefings

Settings:

Dessert receptions in homes of members, box lunches in office conference rooms, One-on-One Points of Entry in people's offices or homes

Top Three FAQs:

- With all the scary information I read about the state of our rainforests, isn't it too late to make a difference?
- What is your organization doing specifically to turn the situation around?
- What evidence do you have of success?

Top Three Facts:

- ___ % of the world's rain forests are endangered.
- Our most vital medicines come from the rainforest.
- We are losing ___ % or our rainforest daily.

Essential Story:

Family in the rainforest no longer having to cut down trees in order to earn a living. "I hated to ruin God's beautiful earth."

Format:

1. **CAPTURE NAMES:** Sign-in list has been prepared in advance based on RSVPs. People check off their names on the list and make any corrections in the contact information listed.

2. **WELCOME:** Host (the person whose home or office the event takes place in)

3. **VISIONARY LEADER TALK:** Executive Director

   a. Why I do this

   b. How the problem has changed since I started working in this field

   c. Urgent need to take action now

   d. Success stories

   e. Where we need to be in ten years, and how we plan to get there

4. **EMOTIONAL HOOK:** How the Essential Story and other stories will be told

   a. Video of the rainforest, interviews with native people, scientists, volunteers

   b. Photo album from a recent trip to the rainforest sitting on the coffee table for people to look through during the social time before the program begins

c. Live testimonial from a volunteer who was on the recent trip to the rainforest. Tells what she saw, how the trip changed her life. Reads a letter or shows an artifact she received from one of the native women she met on the trip.

EXAMPLE 4

Faith-based retirement home Sunday afternoon Point of Entry.

Design Concerns:

- Nursing homes are "depressing"—people will not want to come to a Point of Entry on-site.
- The key audience—family members—is comprised of working people who will not make a special trip to the retirement home during the week.
- Family members may already be contributing financially to their parents' care; will be offended to come to a "fundraising event."

Solution:

Name of Point of Entry:

Sunday Lunch

Setting:

The lawn outside the dining room of the retirement center on Sundays for lunch

Top Three FAQs:

- Why do you need money anyway? We already pay so much to have our parents here.
- What are your plans for growth/expansion?
- Why is there so much staff turnover?

Top Three Facts:

- We are not covering our full costs from the resident fee alone. The true cost of providing the quality care we offer is $ ___ versus the monthly fee to be a resident of only $ ___.

- Average number of years of stay has increased to ___. Many of our residents run out of their own resources sooner than they expected. We don't want to have to ask them to move out at this point in their lives.

- Staffing shortages are critical. Turnover is over ___% a year. The only way we can keep good people is to pay competitively. This fundraising effort helps avoid raising the monthly resident fees.

Essential Story:

Son talking about the peace of mind knowing his mother is being loved and well taken care of in this faith-based setting.

Format:

1. **CAPTURE NAMES:** Sign in table with individual cards

2. **WELCOME:** Board Chair

   a. Invocation: Pastor

3. **VISIONARY LEADER TALK:** CEO

   a. Highlight the needs

   b. The story about my own mother

4. **EMOTIONAL HOOK:** How the Essential Story and other stories will be told

   a. Testimonial from son: Essential Story

   b. Testimonial from staff person about the anxiety of a resident who depleted her financial reserves and was worried about being put out of the home

   c. Optional tour of the new medical clinic

EXAMPLE 5

Large (on-site) high-end Point of Entry for research department of major university.

Design Concerns:

- Making research funding seem urgent while in a comfortable university setting, i.e. looking "needy" enough.
- Explaining complex research projects to lay people.
- Guests are local people in the community, not necessarily alumni.

Solution:

Name of Point of Entry:

The Keys to the Future

Setting:

University Health Sciences conference room and classrooms

Top Three FAQs:

- Why does a big university like this need my money for research? I thought you had big government grants to fund that work.
- Isn't research just a big black hole to fund? Does it ever end? Do we ever really find what we're looking for?
- How would my support benefit real people like me who have suffered from that disease?

Top Three Facts:

- This university has produced major research in the last ten years, which has contributed to the cures for _____ .
- We have ___% of the world's finest scientists in the fields of _____ and _____ .

- Our main sources of research funding—ten years ago and now: (pie chart).

Essential Story:

Young woman or man saved due to research finding that led to a special treatment or medication. "Thank you for saving my life."

Format:

1. **CAPTURE NAMES:** Sign-in tables with pre-printed name tags based on contact info collected earlier in the RSVP process

2. **WELCOME:** Trustee or regent of the university who is involved with Health Sciences

3. **VISIONARY LEADER TALK:** Head of Health Sciences Division

    a. This university is the center of some of the most critical research going on in the country right now. We have already made huge advances in _____ . Today you will have a chance to meet some of our outstanding researchers and learn about their work firsthand.

    b. We appreciate the support from the leaders of our local community

4. **EMOTIONAL HOOK:** How the Essential Story and other stories will be told

    a. Breakout sessions with four researchers, each on a different topic (guests choose one): cancer, heart disease, diabetes, Alzheimer's. Each describes their research briefly and what medical advances have already been made in their field thanks to similar research.

    b. Some video or slides

    c. Personal testimonial if appropriate from the researcher or testimonial from another person who has benefited from cancer research, etc.

       d. Researchers tell their dreams of what they hope to accomplish with their work, and discuss funding challenges

5. Luncheon for all guests with speech by president of the university

EXAMPLE 6

Point of Entry in a Box for a national social justice or advocacy organization.

Design Concerns:
- No one from the "head office" will be present at the Points of Entry. Materials need to stand alone.
- Mission of the organization is broad and not hands-on. Concern that Emotional Hook is difficult to convey.

Solution:
Name of Point of Entry:
Listen Up, Speak Up!

Setting:
Homes of members or supporters

Top Three FAQs:
- What is social justice? How do you define social injustice?
- What can we/you really do to make a difference? How can you change the way people think and behave?
- How do we broaden our base of supporters—rather than just having the people who believe in this keep talking only amongst ourselves?

Top Three Facts:
- Social Injustice is prevalent in our society, in every community. Research has shown that the root of social injustice is lack of communication. People need to talk to each other about real issues. Our programs seek to establish dialog between people.

- Our top three programs are:
  - Dine-around diversity dinners
  - In-school programs
  - Media awareness program
- Here are some of the results of our programs:
  - ___# of children educated
  - ___# of adults attending "Dialog Dinners"
  - ___% decrease in the number of racial incidents in our community

Essential Story:

School kids in the playground. Discriminatory incident. One child comes to the defense of another, using principles they learned in one of our classes.

Format:

1. **CAPTURE NAMES:** Check-in person at front door or at kitchen table; sign-in cards

2. **WELCOME:** Host or hostess (person whose house the event is being held in)

3. **VISIONARY LEADER TALK:** Host

   a. Why this is so important to me

   b. My personal story of social injustice

   c. My decision to devote my life to eradicating this problem

   d. Progress made to date

   e. The gap that still needs to be filled

   f. Our top priorities

4. **EMOTIONAL HOOK:** How the Essential Story and other stories will be told

   a. Video: National video showing key programs with several testimonials

   b. Live testimonial: Person who has attended one of the discussion dinners says how it changed her life and how the training materials have been useful in talking with her children. Tells of her commitment to a better world for the next generation.

EXAMPLE 7

Take-it-on-the-road Point of Entry for a statewide rural primary health care program.

Design Concerns:

- Population is widely dispersed geographically.
- Total population is small.
- There is no physical location; services are provided in mobile vans.

Solution:

Develop local advisory group of ten members in each town. Have them each agree to host one Point of Entry or co-host with another advisory group member.

Name of Point of Entry:

Healthy and Happy!

Setting:

Community centers, church halls, restaurants. Each host selects the venue where people in that community regularly gather. Van is parked outside.

Top Three FAQs:

- How often do you come to our town?
- What if I have emergency needs in the interim?
- What does the money you raise go towards?

Top Three Facts:

- We have been in existence for twenty years; traveling around the state providing services to ___ number of communities in our van. We have served over ___ people of all ages and all income levels.

- We have a highly qualified staff—Certified Registered Nurses and Nurse Practitioners, who are capable of treatment and reference for more complex medical problems to hospital, if needed.

- No charge for services; contributions are accepted. Only ___% of our services are government-funded.

Essential Story:

Mother afraid to bring in child for fear of more serious illness. Friends told her how nice the nurse was. Child treated on the spot and "cured." Mother's minor medical problems treated as well.

Format:

1. **CAPTURE NAMES:** Sign-in table with local greeter; individual sign-in cards

2. **WELCOME:** Local advisory board member

3. **VISIONARY LEADER TALK:** Local advisory board member

   a. How I got involved

   b. What a difference this program has made in our community

   c. How many more people we still are turning away

   d. We would like to double the number of health van days here

4. **EMOTIONAL HOOK:** How the Essential Story and other stories will be told

   a. Nurse reading letter from happy patient

   b. Live testimonial from happy patient

   c. Photo display set up on table (photos provided by the state program office)

   d. Tour of the van with simulated case example to "show off" all the supplies and equipment

EXAMPLE 8

Rehearsal Point of Entry for a performing arts organization (theater, chorus, opera, symphony, dance).

Design Concerns:

- How to convey an Emotional Hook for an arts organization?
- How to convey financial needs to people who are members and arts patrons. They "joined" to get season tickets and good parking at events.
- No fancy meeting space. Just rehearsal and performance space.

Solution:

Name of Point of Entry:

Behind the Curtain

Setting:

Director's office, lunchroom or rehearsal space. Scheduled to coincide with a rehearsal.

Top Three FAQs:

- Why do you need money? Don't I already pay enough in ticket fees?
- Why aren't you doing a better job of marketing your programs? I still see empty seats here from time to time at performances. If you sold out every night, wouldn't that mean you would have enough money?
- Are the performers all union-wage employees making big salaries?

Top Three Facts:

- Ticket price only covers ___% of the total cost to put on each performance. We need to raise the rest from the community. Even if we sold out each performance, we would still need to raise $___. Our average performer makes $___ per show.

- Our attendance has increased to ___% over the past two years. We put on ___ number of shows per season. Each one takes ___ hours and weeks and months of preparation. We would love to be able to offer an additional performance this year on _____.

- We also offer in-school educational programs to foster music/dance/theater appreciation in children. Last year alone, we taught programs to ___ students right here in our community.

Essential Story:

A patron's testimonial about a particularly brilliant performance: "I always feel stimulated and inspired when I leave here. I am lifted out of my day-to-day world."

Format:

1. **CAPTURE NAMES:** Sign-in table at front door; individual sign-in cards

2. **WELCOME:** Board chair or key arts patron

3. **VISIONARY LEADER TALK:** Executive Director

   a. The short history of this theater

   b. Where we'd like to be in five years

4. **EMOTIONAL HOOK:** How the Essential Story and other stories will be told

a. Artistic Director tells about why they love their work; gives one example of a day in the life of one of the performers. He/She highlights why the performers love their work in the face of the many challenges they may face, and briefs the guests on the content of the show they will be rehearsing today.

b. Guests invited to come into the performance room/theater to stay for as much of the rehearsal as they would like.

EXAMPLE 9

Volunteer-led drive-around Point of Entry for Habitat for Humanity.

Design Concerns:

- No office space big enough to meet in.
- No paid staff.
- How to convey the impact of the organization's work on the lives of the volunteers and the "partner families" who are selected to receive a Habitat home.

Solution:

Name of Point of Entry:

Habitour

Setting:

Meet at Habitat warehouse and board bus for tour.

Top Three FAQs:

- How do you select the families who receive a Habitat house?
- What are the demographics of the families selected? Are they all unemployed?
- What conditions are the houses in when the families move out?

Top Three Facts:

- Home ownership has been shown to be the most significant predictor of stable family life.
- The average cost of a modest home in our community is $___. That would require a down payment of $___ and monthly payments of $___. That means the total wages in that family would need to be at least $___ per month, just to cover the payments.

- Habitat for Humanity does not just give away houses. The families selected must be working and able to make the monthly mortgage payments. Their down payments are forgiven over time based on the sweat equity they must contribute to building the house.

Essential Story:

The moment of a Habitat house dedication: The parents are overwhelmed with gratitude when given the keys and the Bible for their new home.

Format:

1. **CAPTURE NAMES:** Table at entrance to warehouse; people fill out cards before boarding the tour bus

2. **WELCOME:** On the bus by board member

3. **VISIONARY LEADER TALK:** By lead volunteer while driving to the first stop on the tour

    a. Explains the work of Habitat for Humanity

    b. What the tour will cover

    c. Why he personally enjoys volunteering

4. **EMOTIONAL HOOK:** How the Essential Story and other stories will be told.

    a. First stop: Drive by a typical "before" home of a Habitat homeowner. Point out the neighborhood surroundings, how far to the nearest school and other key points.

    b. Second stop: A Habitat "build" in progress. Everyone gets off the bus to witness the building process firsthand. Live testimonial from one volunteer about the impact of this volunteer experience.

c. Back on the bus, joined by future homeowner (who has been working at the build site all morning). She tells her story: Working family with four children. Had been living in a one-room "house." Children could not study. Poor lighting, no heat. Parents could not get ahead. After they move into their new house, kids doing better at school, so proud to be able to bring a friend home after school. Parents taking classes at local college—career advancement.

d. Drive by site of future Habitat house(s). Lead volunteer tells of plans for what will be built there.

5. Arrive back at starting point. Total lapsed time: one hour.

EXAMPLE 10

Role-play Point of Entry for job placement program for people with physical disabilities.

Design Concerns:

- Small office.
- Clients rarely present.
- Nothing to show at office; most work takes place at vocational technical schools or at community centers.

Solution.

Name of Point of Entry:

A Day in the Life

Setting:

Meeting room in small office

Top Three FAQs:

- What kind of jobs do you find for these people?
- How do your clients get to the job interviews?
- How are they accepted in the work environment?

Top Three Facts:

- Within six months of entering our program, ___% of our clients are placed in jobs commensurate with their training and skills, spanning all industries and skill levels.
- We teach people interview skills and life skills necessary to both get and keep a good job.
- Our clients are regularly acknowledged as being "just another person on the team." They're helping to break down the stereotypes about what it means to be fully employed as a person with a physical disability.

Essential Story:

Thirty-eight-year-old man, former construction worker, now confined to wheelchair after on-the-job spinal cord injury, retrained as computer programmer. Tells what it meant to him to get his new job. Wife tells about the impact on her and their two young children.

Format:

1. **CAPTURE NAMES:** Sign-in at table (all greeters are in wheelchairs)

2. **WELCOME:** Former board member

3. **VISIONARY LEADER TALK:** Executive Director

   a. Tells the story of his own disability

   b. Tells how he attended a similar program in another state and how that program changed his life

   c. Shares his dream for others to have access to job training, job placement and support

4. **EMOTIONAL HOOK:** How the Essential Story and other stories will be told

   a. Each guest is given a job placement card that describes the true situation of a person whose identity they will take on for the next hour

   b. They are asked to sit in a wheelchair for the entire Point of Entry

   c. The Job Placement Coordinator conducts a mock interview skills class, asking each of the guests to speak up— in character—as she poses one or two interview questions to each of them

5. The last ten minutes are spent debriefing so that the guests can talk about what they learned from the experience

EXAMPLE 11

Online Point of Entry for international relief organization.

Design Concerns:

- Programs and donors all over the world; programs are wide-ranging, such as meals, shelter, lending, health education. Feels large, complicated and impersonal.

- The only way people can experience the work firsthand is to travel overseas to visit the programs.

- Perception that the organization already has plenty of funding. How could one donor's small gift make a difference in such a big organization?

Solution:

Name of Point of Entry:

Extend a Hand

Setting:

The organization's Web site: Guests attend the Point of Entry online, at their own convenience.

Top Three FAQs:

- What are the top three programs you offer around the world?

- Which of those programs is offered in the country I am most interested in?

- What kinds of work is the organization doing there? How is it changing lives?

Top Three Facts:

- We are a humanitarian organization dedicated to empowering local leaders and groups to improve their lives. We work side-by-side with local groups and leaders to offer our programs. We only offer the programs they request. Therefore, the programs differ from area to area.

- For example, in one country in Africa we may offer basic education program for girls. In another, we teach agricultural techniques.

- Our microcredit program gives small loans to women and provides support in using that money for women and their families to rise out of poverty.

Essential Story:

Indigenous woman who receives a loan of $50, starts a basket-making business, buys books for her children, buys a cow, now can feed and educate family.

Format:

1. **CAPTURE NAMES:** Sign in on Web site at the end of the Point of Entry tour

2. **WELCOME:** Message with photo from national board chair

3. **VISIONARY LEADER TALK:** Executive Director or Founder

   a. Tells a story illustrated on the Web site

   b. Brief streaming video

   c. Includes map of all sites around the world, which guests can click on to learn more

4. **EMOTIONAL HOOK:** How the Essential Story and other stories will be told

   a. Guest can click through to the country and type of program of interest

   b. They can click to specific testimonial stories with photos

   c. Stories are told succinctly in the person's own words

   d. May include photos, streaming video and sound

EVENTS

CHAPTER 12

FOUR TYPES OF EVENTS

Once you have taken the time to design the elements of your Point of Entry presentation, you will see ways to insert this mission-focused material into every other event you offer. This will enable you to convert many of your more labor-intensive, stand-alone special events into events that can forward your system for building lifelong donors.

The purpose of this section on events is for you to be able to do just that—to categorize and redesign, if necessary, each of your events so that they fit together into a carefully crafted system of annual events which you can leave as a legacy for your organization. Please be forewarned: over time, adopting the Raising More Money approach is likely to put an end to many of your one-year-at-a-time, "fundraising fluff" special events and grow deeper relationships with your donors.

Before we can decide how to convert many of your existing events, we need to step back and review the Raising More Money classification of events. In our model for building a self-sustaining individual giving program, any event your organization is now putting on can easily be recast to fit into one of the following four categories:

- A Point of Entry Event in a Box
- A Point of Entry Conversion Event
- A Free One-Hour Ask Event
- A Free Feel-Good Cultivation Event (also known as a Point of Re-Entry)

Start by making a list of all the events your organization currently puts on each year. Include all types of events: annual dinners, holiday parties, volunteer and donor recognition events, anniversary events, golf tournaments, walk-a-thons, theater events, black tie galas, auctions. You can even include volunteer recruitment events, training classes or actual performances of your arts organization.

CONVERTING YOUR CURRENT EVENTS

Now let's define the four types of events you could convert them to.

1. Point of Entry Events in a Box

The first type of event is the Point of Entry in a Box—that generic repeatable event you could leave as a legacy to your organization. Imagine if you could actually take some of the events you are now working diligently to produce and turn them into your regularly scheduled Point of Entry Events. Without having to invent a whole new series of events, you could jump-start your Point of Entry program quickly.

By now, you are familiar with the three essential ingredients of our stand-alone Point of Entry Event: Facts 101, the Emotional Hook, and being able to Capture the Names of the guests with their permission. Guests who attend these events are usually invited word-of-mouth by a friend and are coming for the sole purpose of learning more about your organization. The content of the introductory session is so generic you could put it in a box and take it to someone's home or office, in addition to presenting it at your own site.

Think about which of your existing events may already meet these requirements or could easily be modified to do so. The best contenders are well-attended program-related events that repeat weekly or monthly; for example, tours, orientations or open houses you may offer for new volunteers, staff or members, for example. Odds are, with only a slight bit of tweaking, you could have a ready-made Point of Entry.

The one criterion that is trickiest to meet is that the guests need to know in advance that they are coming to an introductory session about your organization, as opposed to coming to a more specific volunteer training or lecture on a particular topic or an open house. For example, a retirement home we worked with had been holding regular Sunday afternoon open houses for family members and potential new residents. After adopting the Raising More Money Model, it was easy for them to add a thirty-minute sit-down Point of Entry "meeting." Rather than having to organize a whole new set of events, they merely added (and publicized) this more formal component to an already popular and well-attended event in their community.

No doubt, your organization has other existing events that could qualify as natural Points of Entry, with only slight modifications.

2. Point of Entry Conversion Events

The second type of event is what we call a Point of Entry Conversion Event. Distinct from the standard Point of Entry in a Box, these conversion events are usually the ones we call "fundraisers." It is fine to charge people money to come to a Point of Entry Conversion Event; just be sure that all of the objectives of a standard Point of Entry in a Box have been covered before they leave.

Here is a little test of whether your event qualifies as a Point of Entry for your guests: The next day, if someone had asked them about the dinner-dance or the golf tournament, could the guests have answered the following two-question pop quiz?

Question 1: What was the name of the organization for which the event was raising funds?

While they may well remember how much they enjoyed the golf or the dinner-dance, will they be able to recall the name of the organization that worked so hard to produce the event and ultimately received their financial support?

Question 2: What does that organization do?

Even if your name is well known in your community, do not
assume that people truly know about the breadth of your programs. What people will remember most is a video or short
testimonial from someone who has benefited from your work.

In other words, you will need to insert a Point of Entry element
into the sit-down portion of your fundraising event. This should
include a short Visionary Leader Talk with facts and emotion plus a
brief, live testimonial from a person whose life has been changed
thanks to the work of your organization. This can all be accomplished
in ten minutes, with good preparation.

It almost goes without saying that you need to Capture the
Names with the guests' permission. At most of these events, such as
auctions or golf tournaments, you should have a natural way to know
who will be coming in advance. Do not assume that this means you
have their permission to follow up after the event. For that explicit
permission, you need to ask people, at some point during the event,
to let you know that they would like you to contact them. The
easiest way to do this is by placing a card under their lunch or
dinner plate or in the center of their table. The emcee needs to refer
to the card and encourage people to fill it out and leave it with their
table host if they would like to speak directly with someone from
the organization.

Do you have good records of the names and phone numbers of
their guests? Moreover, would you have a legitimate reason for calling them after the event to find out what they thought of it? Or
would that seem too contrived? What could you add to the event
that would let those guests who might want more information identify themselves so you would have sufficient permission to follow up
with them?

3. Free One-Hour Ask Events

The third event is our formula Free One-Hour Ask Event. While other events resemble this, most organizations are not yet doing the type of event we are referring to here.

To qualify as a Free One-Hour Ask Event in this model, the guests are invited verbally by a friend who serves as a Table Captain to a free breakfast or lunch event.

The guests know in advance that they will be asked to give money at the event. The Table Captain also must be sure to inform them at the point of the invitation that there is "no minimum and no maximum gift" expected. As much as anything, you are asking them to come and learn more about the organization. It will be your job to inspire and educate them so they will want to give.

The Free One-Hour Ask Event is ideally suited to the new fundraising reality because it provides a straightforward, time-limited infomercial about the outstanding work of your organization. In one tightly choreographed hour, this event provides the Facts, the Emotional Hook and a compelling Ask for multiple-year support at specific giving levels.

This event is an extremely effective money raiser for the following reasons:

1. The majority of guests have already attended a "real" Point of Entry Event and have been followed-up with personally and involved. They serve as a critical mass within the larger group and provide a momentum towards giving.

2. The guests have been well prepared in advance and know that making a contribution will be optional at the event. You must base your financial projections on the assumption that only half of the guests will give at all. Then you may be pleasantly surprised.

3. The event is free. To repeat: In fundraising, "free" is magical. If you were to charge even $10 a person to attend this event, it would never be as successful. People are given a nice, basic breakfast or lunch, for which they do not feel

overly obligated. They are free to enjoy themselves and to give freely when asked, if they so choose. Do not do this event as a dinner. Dinner implies a greater degree of obligation, which could get in the way of donors choosing freely how much they would like to give.

We will go into more detail about the Free One-Hour Ask Event in Chapter 16.

4. Free Feel-Good Cultivation Events (also known as Points of Re-Entry)

Fourth and finally comes the Free Feel-Good Cultivation Event. The name pretty much says it all. These are the "reward" events for your Multiple-Year Giving Society donors that reconnect them to the Emotional Hook and reinforce the wisdom of their investment in your organization. That means these events always include a program or theme that ties to your mission.

Do not underestimate the magic of a "free" event. If you inspire them, people will remember you gave them something for free when it comes time to ask them for the next contribution. Just make sure you have one or more underwriters who receive plenty of credit, so your loyal donors will know you did not spend any of their money to pay for this event.

To keep it simple, you can invite donors to internal events already planned to honor your clients or families such as graduations, show-and-tell nights, special theater performances or expert lectures.

Free Feel-Good Cultivation Events can be varied for donors at different giving levels. You may invite your biggest donors to an elegant dinner at the most exclusive private home or with a revered person in your field, if that is the sort of thing they would like. Your smaller Multiple-Year Donors might be invited to a dinner or lecture series, a family picnic or a special "environmental day" or "peace day." Free Feel-Good Events may also be used as Points of Entry to introduce insiders to the next dream for the organization, especially a major gifts campaign or endowment.

Unlike Point of Entry Conversion Events, mentioned above, these Free Feel-Good Cultivation Events are not aimed at attracting new friends to the organization, but rather towards cultivating your inner circle of Multiple-Year Donors. Of course, these insiders are always encouraged to bring friends to these Free Feel-Good Cultivation Events as well; so long as the focus of the event really is on your loyal prior donors.

Finally, just as with a Point of Entry Event, a Point of Re-Entry always engenders a Follow-Up Call, eliciting more feedback, which in turn enables you to further customize your approach to each donor. This keeps the donor going around the cycle with you. We will discuss Free Feel-Good Cultivation Events in more detail in Chapter 17.

SOME SOUL-SEARCHING QUESTIONS ABOUT YOUR SPECIAL EVENTS

Before we look at inserting a Point of Entry element into your existing events, let's put each event through some careful scrutiny. Take the time now, while you are alone, without the influence of your staff, board or event committee, to answer these questions honestly for each of the events your organization currently produces.

1. *What have you said to justify not reaching your dollar goal for this event?*
    Do any of the following statements sound familiar?
    "At least we made the board and volunteers happy."
    "We had no other choice; everyone expects us to put on this event; it's an annual tradition."
    "It's an opportunity to get our name out there in the community."
    "It lets us tell our story to a broader group of people."
    "It's a 'friend' raiser."
    Most of the time, these kinds of statements justify the fact that, in spite of your best efforts, you don't know how to have the event make more money.

2.   *What is the real reason for having the event, anyway?*
     This may not be the "official" reason you tell the world, but
     what would insiders say is the real reason you are having this
     event? Is it because no one could say no to the board chair or a
     key volunteer? Is it just the habitual thing to do?

3.   *Is there really an expectation this event will raise money?*
     If so, is the stated fundraising goal for the event different from
     the amount you absolutely must raise from the event? Is every-
     one expecting it will raise the amount you put in the budget?

4.   *How attached are you to the form of this event—annual din-
     ner, auction, etc.?*
     How attached are the others who are involved? Do they know
     the facts about how little it nets for the amount of work it takes
     to produce?

5.   *What if someone just walked in and wrote you a check for your
     total dollar goal? Would you still have the event?*
     Pretend for a moment, that you alone had the power to cancel
     each event forever. If you knew you had the money goal cov-
     ered, which ones would you discontinue?

6.   *Thinking ahead to your next big event, if you don't make your
     goal, what will be the reason?*
     It is interesting to notice you probably already know what the
     reasons and excuses will be, yet continue to go through the
     motions.

7.   *If the event is supposed to be a fundraiser, do you know how
     much it actually nets?*
     Has anyone actually calculated the true costs, adding in all the
     staff costs in addition to volunteer time and the obvious hard
     costs?

8. *How many volunteers did it really take to put the event on?*
   Did you burn them out or make them happy? Are they bored with the event? Would they rather have hosted a smaller gathering and have you and a "testimonial person" come and tell your story? Would they rather have just given you a check and skipped the event altogether?

9. *If you have dedicated fundraising staff, what else could they have been doing with the same amount of time and energy to bring in more money than this event nets?*
   For example, what if they spent the same number of hours making calls or visits to major donors? What might that have yielded?

10. *For how many months in advance have you and your team been obsessing about the event?*
    What about the terror the weeks and days before the event approaches, or the fear of whether you will even make the break-even number, assuming you know what that number is?

11. *Speaking of break even, do you know from the beginning you have big fixed costs to meet?*
    These are things like theater ticket sales, pricey food costs, audio/visual equipment, and room rental costs—anything you couldn't get donated.

12. *Is this the right kind of event for your organization?*
    Is it consistent with your mission? How could it showcase your mission even more? Is it the best way to tell your organization's story?

13. *Does this type of event give you enough predictors of the results?*
    Are there enough benchmarks along the way to let you adjust accordingly in advance if you have fewer Table Captains or tickets sold?

14. *What would you think if you had to sit through that program?*
    Do people really care about the speaker? Is the speaker's message even relevant to your organization or is the speaker just there to draw in more guests? If the latter, then how many more people will that speaker attract? How much more in the bottom line? Will that extra revenue more than cover the speaker's fees? What is the likelihood those guests who come just to hear this speaker will ever become lifelong donors?

15. *What are you building for future years by having this event?*
    Where does this event fit into your overall individual giving program?

16. *On a scale of 1-10, how excited are you about producing this event?*
    You will need to be the cheerleader in those inevitable stressful days between now and event day. Your enthusiasm and commitment to the success of the event will be needed to carry the team forward. If you are not truly excited about what this event will accomplish for your organization, it may be time to speak up now.

Designing your System of Events

Now that you understand the event classification within the Raising More Money Model and have asked, and hopefully answered, many of these soul-searching questions about your current events, you should be ready to design your system.

Using the following Converting Existing Events worksheet, list out all of your current events. Now make your plan for what type of event you would like to convert them to over time. Also begin to plot out on a calendar the ideal time of year for each event if you were starting from scratch.

| Current Events: | Converting Existing Events | | | | |
| | Convert Event To: | | | | Ideal Month |
	Point of Entry	Point of Entry Conversion	Free Feel-Good Cultivation Event	Free One-Hour Ask Event	
1					
2					
3					
4					
5					
6					
7					
8					
9					
10					

Ultimately, what you are aiming to design is what we call a System of Events—a lasting short list of events that build on each other throughout the year, providing each donor or potential donor with precisely the number and quality of event contacts they might like.

For starters, I recommend the following: One Point of Entry Event per month, one Free One-Hour Ask Event per year, two Cultivation Events per year (one for your highest level donors and the other for all your Multiple-Year Donors) and as few Point of Entry Conversion Events as possible. These Conversion Events, especially the ones that have been your most labor-intensive "fundraisers," should be put through the scrutiny of the soul-searching questions, and you will need to make a recommendation as to which ones are worth the effort and should be sustained long-term as part of your system, and which ones should not.

Do not be discouraged in this process. It may take two to three years before you can rotate events to a different time of year or phase them out altogether, if that is your objective. Your purpose now is to design the ideal System of Events that you will be leaving as a legacy.

All events should work together to support each other. For example, if you decide with your team that you will be putting on the Free One-Hour Ask Event every year in either the spring or fall, you will want your main Free Feel-Good Cultivation Event to take place in the opposite season. The first year, you might have more than one event crowded into the same season because you have already announced that date or had the invitations printed, yet by next year you could rotate that event to another part of the year.

The time and thought you put into designing this System of Events will be well worth the effort.

If you have taken the time to tell the truth about each of your events, you should have a good sense of which ones you are committed to keeping or dropping. We have one more issue to consider before we look at redesigning your events: Follow-Up.

CHAPTER 13

PLANNING EVENTS:
BEGIN WITH THE FOLLOW-UP

Although it seems counter-intuitive, the first thing to consider as you redesign each of your events to grow your base of lifelong donors is the Follow-Up. This is true whether the event is destined to become a Point of Entry, a Free Feel-Good Cultivation Event or a Free One-Hour Ask Event. You must plan the entire event working backwards from your plan for follow-up.

What is it about your organization that you want the guests to remember? What will you want them to say when they receive their personal Follow-Up Call?

HAVE YOU CAPTURED THE NAMES WITH PERMISSION?

The first question to ask is how you will decide which of the guests you can legitimately follow up with without it feeling too pushy. What will be your tracking system at the event for identifying people who really would like to stay in contact with you? How will they let you know that you have their permission to contact them?

The easiest and most up-front method is to have some sort of reply card the guests can fill out and give back to a designated person, ideally their table host, indicating they would like more information about your program. While this is clearly the most straightforward, even those guests who are very interested may be reluctant to be the only person at their table who is filling out such a card.

Another approach that works well is to have the emcee, or some other key person who is part of the official program, tell the audience, after the Facts and Emotional Hook have been presented, something like this:

"While we know that most of you just came today to play golf (or dance or whatever), you may have discovered during our program that you have an interest in learning more about our work. There is a person seated at each table who is very familiar with our organization. For today, they are serving as our experts. Would that person at each table please raise your hands now so we can all see who you are? (Emcee pauses while hands go up and everyone looks around.) Feel free to talk with them and let them know you'd like more information. We would be delighted to have someone from the organization talk with you further."

That kind of a statement sets you up pretty well to capture the next tier of interested guests.

Of course, you give these designated experts special ribbons on their nametags and make a big fuss about them. Let them know in advance that you are counting on them to circulate and talk to as many people as they can during the event. Tell them you will be calling them to debrief the day after the event. They should be on their toes during the entire event.

A third approach is to get a little bolder and think about who you could call quite naturally even if they did not give you explicit permission to do so. If any of the guests were prior "insiders"— donors, volunteers or board members—you may have enough implicit permission to call them randomly and ask for their frank feedback about the event. Also ask them about any other comments or reactions they heard from other guests. They will be flattered that you considered them enough of an insider to call.

A fourth strategy is to review the various categories of guests in terms of their past association with your organization, such as former board members, former volunteers, or former staff, in terms of the role they played in the event, and then to call two or three key people in each category to help you with your "random follow-up survey." While it is a bit contrived, people will be impressed you are taking the time to solicit their input and most will be delighted to talk with you. As you listen to their responses, see if you can sniff out any trends you might want to pursue with a telephone or e-mail campaign to a broader group of attendees.

Lastly, consider the guests who said they wanted to attend but did not attend. How could you legitimately follow up with them? If a personal phone call seems like too much, could you send them a copy of the video with a "we missed you" note from their friend?

Everyone who will be involved in the follow-up process needs to be well set-up from the beginning. They are your special agents during the event. Deputize your board members and long-term supporters. Have them keep their antennae up.

WHAT KIND OF FOLLOW-UP AND WHEN?

The main secret of follow-up in the new reality is timing.

The two weeks after each event are, by far, the most fertile time for additional fundraising as well as cultivation. Unfortunately, by the time the actual event happens, most event organizers are burned out and exhausted. Your guests, on the other hand, are just getting interested. Now is the time they are curious and eager to learn more. Tell your event planners and key development staff not to schedule their vacations until at least two weeks after the event! Otherwise they will miss the delayed positive results of their work.

In terms of the type of follow-up, no doubt you have already thought of the obvious: letters. Most organizations have gotten the thank-you letter down to an art form. It is a beautifully crafted letter, personally signed by the perfect person. Ideally suited to the pace of the old reality, it arrives a week or two after the event. While this is fine for the formal IRS-required response, letters will not get you that timely, open-ended feedback you need.

Your first choice for follow-up should be by telephone because it provides immediate, voice-to-voice, real-time dialog. Although many of your donors may prefer e-mail, for the majority of donors nothing yet substitutes for a phone call or a voice mail message left within three days of the event, while the afterglow is still warm. This call or message thanks the person for coming and asks for their feedback, again engaging them directly with a real person associated with your organization. Yes, it is fine to leave a voice mail or send an e-mail message. Let them know how to reach you and be prepared to call them two more times to actually connect with them.

All of this phone contact presumes that you did an impeccable job of Capturing the Names and phone numbers of the guests at your event. If the event was well done, they will have left inspired and educated. In other words, they should still remember you. Since many of them gave someone their names to be called, they will have been looking forward to hearing from you.

WHO IS THE BEST PERSON TO MAKE THE FOLLOW-UP CALL?

The best person to make the Follow-Up Call is someone very closely connected to your organization. Ideally this person is someone the guest met at the event, even in passing, who will be their ongoing contact over the next few years, their Donor Services Representative. In many cases, this will be one high-level staff person or a long-time volunteer who single-handedly does all the follow-up. This provides consistency for your guests.

I recommend not having guests followed up with by their personal friends, other than as a courtesy thank-you call. This "official" Follow-Up Call should be done by someone closer to the inside of the organization, yet at arms-length from the guests so they have the freedom to give more direct feedback.

The only exception to this is in the case of a very large event where a large number of guests will be receiving Follow-Up Calls. Then you will need several callers. In this case, assemble your best team and train them to make the official Follow-Up Calls.

THE POST-EVENT FOLLOW-UP CALL

Be sure that each caller is following the same script or outline of general questions you want to have covered. This will ensure consistency. Also be sure they have a standardized way of recording the information so it can be entered into your database right away.

Here is a basic script of what you will want to cover in the post-event Follow-Up Call. You can modify the exact wording to fit your situation.

1. Thank the person for coming to the event. Let them know your organization is honored they made it a priority to be there.

2. Ask them what they thought about the event. What did they like most about it? Do they feel they learned anything new about the organization? What suggestions would they have for changes or improvements?

3. Is there any way they might like to become more involved with the organization? If they have already been involved, listen carefully here for signs of renewed or increased interest.

4. Is there anyone who came to mind during the event they would suggest you contact or invite to a tour or other Point of Entry Event?

5. If they requested any additional information, let them know how you will be providing that. Thank them for taking their time for this call.

Now that you are primed for the Follow-Up, we are ready to consider converting existing fundraising events to Point of Entry Events.

CHAPTER 14

CONVERTING EVENTS TO POINTS OF ENTRY IN A BOX

Wouldn't it be wonderful if your organization were already putting on well-attended, regularly scheduled events that could easily be modified to become Points of Entry in a Box? These events could provide you with a natural venue and ready-made audience of people who have already expressed interest in your work. That sounds like precisely the type of guests you would want to have at your recurring Point of Entry (in a Box) Events.

Therefore, before you launch into creating a whole new series of events for your organization, it is well worth taking the time to scope out existing event contenders. Again, you are looking for mission- or program-focused, repeatable events geared to introducing new people to your programs. These would be your more public "events" such as tours, volunteer recruitment meetings and classes. They may not be events that have been designed for donors or potential donors at all. Yet with the slight addition of our Point of Entry elements, you would be off and running.

The best case for converting these events is that the guests know that they are coming just to learn about something new. In other words, they do not think they are coming to a sporting event, like a golf tournament or a bowl-a-thon. Therefore, you have permission to tell them your story—to educate and inspire them. Depending on the purpose of the gathering in the first place, you may already have even Captured their Names.

For example, the regularly scheduled "build days" of Habitat for Humanity, which builds homes in partnership with the needy families who will be purchasing the homes, can bring out tens or even hundreds of volunteers weekly. For many of these volunteers who sign in and fill out a release of liability form at the beginning of the day, this workday is their first exposure to the organization and they are very curious to learn more. What better place to offer a brief Point of Entry than right there at the construction site?

Many Habitat for Humanity affiliates conduct their Point of Entry in a Box events over lunch on these work days. This is the one time of the day when the morning and afternoon shifts of volunteers overlap. Imagine yourself, having worked hard all morning side by side with other volunteers and the family who will be moving into the house, now sitting outside in the sunshine having a well-deserved lunch. It would be quite natural for the local Visionary Leader—usually the executive director or board chairman of that affiliate—to stand up and share their Visionary Leader Talk followed by the powerful testimonial from one of the family members telling their story and then thanking the volunteers for giving time today to build a house for their family. At the end of that ten minutes, if the board chair or leader were to point out the person who would like to call the volunteers in the next week or so to get their feedback about the work day and to see if they have any further interest in knowing about the organization, many people would be happy to give them feedback.

Similarly, a Red Cross chapter added a regularly scheduled thirty-minute Point of Entry "meeting" before each of their "CPR Saturday" training sessions. They advertised these optional Meet Your American Red Cross sessions in all of their publications and had a built-in resounding turnout each week.

If you work in the performing arts, you are fortunate to have rehearsals that can make natural Point of Entry in a Box Events that would be of great interest to potential supporters. Let the guests know in advance that these regularly scheduled "Behind the Curtain" events will include a backstage briefing on the upcoming performance from the artistic director or conductor, as well as a brief presentation on the other work of the organization.

As you scan your list of existing, recurring events or programs you offer the public, do not be surprised to discover that you have strong contenders that would make easy and natural Points of Entry in a Box.

CHAPTER 15

POINT OF ENTRY CONVERSION EVENTS

Most of the fundraising events you are now working so hard to produce in order to attract new donors can become Point of Entry Conversion Events with relatively little tweaking. Furthermore, if you want to gear the event for your existing donors, and you can get the event fully underwritten so it is free to attend, you will have a Free Feel-Good Cultivation Event. As long as you are going to do the work of bringing people together for events, why not have them leave educated and inspired about your fine programs? Otherwise, what have you built for the future?

Let's review the three essential components of a Point of Entry Event:

1. People get the basic Facts 101 about your organization.

2. They feel the Emotional Hook and connection to your work.

3. You Capture the Names, phone numbers and e-mail addresses, with their permission.

Think of all the events and occasions where you could accomplish those three essential ingredients:

- A black-tie gala
- An awards event or volunteer recognition event
- An anniversary event

- An open-air picnic or concert
- A golf tournament
- A community meeting where you are invited to speak
- One of your standard volunteer orientation meetings
- A concert or arts performance
- A parent orientation night

Let's take something pretty standard like a golf tournament, although this same formula could be adapted to any of the events listed above. Unlike a Point of Entry Event, where people know they have been invited to an introductory educational session about the work of the organization, people coming to a golf tournament are coming to play golf.

As mentioned earlier, in order to qualify as a Point of Entry Conversion Event in our model, any guest who attends the golf tournament must be able to answer two questions the next day. Suppose they are out with a friend who asks about the "charity" golf event the day before. The first question is: "What organization did that event benefit?" In other words, they must be able to remember your name. That is easy for some organizations; for others it is more difficult. The second question their friend might ask the next day is: "What does that organization really do, anyway?" They need to be able to say what you do.

What people will remember most is a story. The best way to accomplish this is to insert a ten-minute Point of Entry element into the program while people are seated, having dinner or lunch. This can be accomplished easily with a seven-minute video or Visionary Leader Talk plus a three-minute live testimonial. At a golf tournament or other entertainment or sports event, you only have enough permission to insert a brief program about your work. After all, people really came because they wanted to play golf.

Here is an example of how you could do this: While everyone is seated, the emcee or board chair gets up and says:

> We know most of you came today for a great day of golf and we hope you've had that. As you know, today's event is a benefit for the _____ Organization, and we here at _____ would not be doing our jobs if we did not take advantage of having you all gathered here today to tell you a little more about our organization.

Then have your Visionary Leader speak or show your seven-minute video. Follow this with a three-minute live testimonial.

Following the testimonial, the emcee gets back up and thanks the testimonial speaker.

> Now, again, we know that many of you may not have known much about this wonderful organization before today. Now that you've heard a little more, if you find you would be interested in receiving more information or visiting the organization to see their work first-hand, please identify yourself to the person at your table who has agreed to serve as an "expert" for today. Would that person please raise their hand now? (Everyone looks around to see who the expert at their table is.) You can give this person your business card and we will give you a call.

If it is an evening event where people often don't have their business cards with them, put a preprinted card under each plate or in the center of the table for interested guests to fill out and give to the table expert.

Those people who give you cards are the only ones with whom you have enough permission to follow up, invite to a Point of Entry Event and take around the cycle.

Perhaps you are already doing a perfect Point of Entry Conversion Event without even recognizing it. If not, the addition of a relatively brief testimonial from someone who has benefited greatly from your programs or services—either in person, on video or delivered by a third person such as a staff member—can be very effective.

One of the keys to a successful Point of Entry Conversion Event is intertwining the Facts, the Emotional Hook and the need so that, before they know it, the audience has had an experience of it all. If you are giving awards, make them brief but moving and chock-full of facts that tie each person's story back to the mission of the organization or to one particular aspect of a program.

A participant in one of our workshops did this brilliantly at a black tie dinner "fundraiser" that honored formerly homeless women who had turned their lives around. The tables had been sold to corporate sponsors, many of whom had given their tickets away to others to fill up the tables. The development director assumed that although the guests were there primarily to attend a lovely dinner, the organization could take ten minutes to tell them about the work of the organization. They started the program with some inspirational words from the emcee, the chief executive officer of the major corporate sponsor of the event. This was followed immediately by a moving video about the organization's work. Then the emcee encouraged people to enjoy their dinner and to spend some time talking with the special guest at their table who was most familiar with the organization—either a board member, volunteer or staff person. He also encouraged them to take a moment to read the "testimonial inserts" in their printed programs.

After dinner came the awards presentations, which had been well-scripted and served as real-life testimonials to these women's extraordinary accomplishments in the face of great obstacles. As each woman was called up to receive her award, she was asked to sit in one of the chairs on the stage. At the end of the awards, all the recipients were asked to stand. Of course, after hearing each woman's story, there was a standing ovation and not a dry eye in the house.

Board members were assigned clusters of tables to visit after the dessert was served. The executive director had briefed the table hosts on the overall objective for the event. "This isn't just a pretty party. We want to be sure every single guest leaves here tonight knowing more about our organization, both the facts and the emotional impact of the work we do." Table Captains, staff and board members all knew in advance that the development staff would call them to

debrief on Monday morning. They knew to be on the lookout for people who expressed a real interest in the cause. And before the evening ended, the emcee invited the guests to leave their business card or let their Table Captain know if they would like more information about the organization.

Within a week, every guest who expressed any sincere interest in the organization had received a Follow-Up Call from the director of development. This was in addition to the standard thank-you call or note that their table host would naturally do.

Many people asked if they could take a tour of the shelter (which became their real Point of Entry Event). Others offered in-kind or cash gifts. Some wanted to host a Point of Entry Event of their own. Because this organization was planning to do a Free One-Hour Ask Event a few months later, they were able to convert many of the black-tie dinner guests to Table Captains for the upcoming Ask Event. The organization raised more than $300,000 at this black-tie gala Point of Entry Conversion Event, as well as generating the passion and commitment that led to many new Table Captains for their bigger Ask Event. Good strategy!

Whether you are trying to convert a golf tournament, a black tie gala or a Rotary meeting presentation to a Point of Entry, remember the third essential ingredient is to Capture the Names of those who want more information. No captured names means no Point of Entry Event. As you can see, these Point of Entry Conversion Events are far less efficient in terms of generating new potential donors, than are the classic Points of Entry in a Box. At the classic Point of Entry, you generally have permission to follow up with everyone who has come and to continue around our circle model for as long as they express interest.

This certainly does not mean you should stop telling your organization's story at those public speaking engagements, like the Rotary or Kiwanis presentations, which are wonderful opportunities to tell your organization's story in the community. Just know that you won't be able to do the one-on-one follow-up necessary to build a lifelong donor. On the other hand, when people come up to you at the end of one of these presentations full of passion for your cause,

be sure to ask for their card and give them yours. You can consider that these people who give you their card have attended a Point of Entry Event. Therefore, you should give them a Follow-Up Call and take them around the cycle if they are truly interested.

CHAPTER 16

THE FREE ONE-HOUR ASK EVENT

The third category of event is the Free One-Hour Ask Event. Although the focus of this book is not on Asking for Money but rather on the Point of Entry, I have included this chapter for three reasons.

First, many people who have only a cursory understanding of the Raising More Money Model confuse this Free One-Hour Ask Event with a classic Point of Entry or Point of Entry in a Box. They rush to the Ask with brand new guests, pressuring them to give before the fruit has ripened naturally.

Second, if you do your Points of Entry systematically, following the steps outlined in the previous chapters and then follow up and cultivate people around the cycle, there will come a point where they are naturally ready to give. In other words, it is important for you to appreciate where all your work is leading.

The very people who have been so inspired at your Points of Entry will happily become your best Table Captains at your Free One-Hour Ask Event. They, in turn, will invite other friends who have also attended your Points of Entry. In addition, because of their genuine enthusiasm for your work, they will be more effective in inviting new people to sit at their table at the Free One-Hour Ask Event. Though these new guests are not in any way expected to give money at the Ask Event, they will be swept up into the critical mass of emotion in the room and will be more inclined to want to come to your traditional Point of Entry Event after the Ask Event.

Third and finally, as you read through the flow of the Free One-Hour Ask Event, you will recognize all the familiar elements of the Point of Entry you have worked so hard to refine and test. Suddenly, all of the fruits of your work will become apparent and you will be richly blessed with the financial rewards your organization wants and needs.

HOW THE EVENT WORKS

The Free One-Hour Ask Event is distinct from all other events. In order to be successful using this format, it is a good idea to put aside all the other events that you may think it resembles and just learn how this event works.

The Free One-Hour Ask Event has a particular formula; there is nothing haphazard about it. The program elements are sequenced to build to a climax at the end of the hour. At that point, the guests have been sufficiently educated and inspired in such a natural and respectful manner that they are able to choose freely whether or not they would like to contribute financially by becoming a part of your organization's Multiple-Year Giving Society.

Far from being a high-pressure, obligatory-giving event, the Free One-Hour Ask Event provides people with an unforgettable, succinct presentation of the extraordinary work of your organization. Your guests will be thanking you for having invited them.

This format is now used for many highly successful events, including one that annually raises over $1 million in one hour. Compared to most events people are now busy producing, this type of event requires significantly less work. The best part about it, besides the bottom line of course, is that the entire hour is spent educating the audience about your programs.

For people who have been to your traditional Point of Entry and have been well followed-up with and cultivated through the process, we could say this event serves as their "Point of Ask." They will be asked to become members of your Multiple-Year Giving Society by pledging to give at specified Units of Service for multiple years.

For new people who have never been to a Point of Entry, this event will be their initial Point of Entry and there is no expectation that they will give at all at this event.

It's Free

Notice first and foremost that in our model the Free One-Hour Ask Event is absolutely free to the guests to attend. There is no ticket price. Furthermore, people know in advance they will be asked to give. Yet they are not required to give at all. There are no minimum and no maximum gifts suggested. People can give nothing.

If people have already paid a ticket price, regardless of how small a price, they will resent being asked to give any additional money at the event. In their minds, they have already given. The price of their ticket was their gift to you. Even in the case of an auction, a raffle or a golf tournament, where donors are getting plenty of tangible goodies in return, most donors will feel any money spent was their contribution to their organization.

Table-Captain Driven

Let's revisit where this event happens in our cycle. You have done your Point of Entry Events. You have followed up, in many cases several times, with the same person. You can identify with the help of your database a core group of people who are passionate about the work of your organization. They may not be the people with the most money or the best contacts, but they love your organization. You call them and ask if they would consider being a Table Captain at your free breakfast (or lunch) fundraising event four to six months from now.

They are flattered yet confused. "Free breakfast fundraising event?" they ask. "Just what does that mean?"

"That's right," you reply. "There's no charge to you as a Table Captain, and no charge to any of your guests for attending. It's absolutely free. Yes, they will be asked to contribute, but there will be no minimum and no maximum. I repeat, no minimum. They can give any amount they like. It will be our job to inspire them to want to give. As much as anything, we want people to come and find out about our organization."

The success of the event relies largely on this personal, word-of-mouth invitation each guest receives from a friend who has agreed to be a Table Captain. While you may supplement these personal invitations with printed invitations to people on your organization's mailing list, the majority of the guests should be coming, ideally, because a friend invited them.

Therefore, every Table Captain must understand the way the event works and feel comfortable that their guests will not be pressured in any way to give.

Take the time to go over the suggested wording to be used by each Table Captain as they invite their guests. Make sure they are clear that people will be asked to give money at the end of the event; however, there is no minimum and no maximum contribution expected. In other words, it is fine for people not to give at all.

Let's say thirty people agree to be Table Captains. The job of each Table Captain is to fill a table of ten for the event. That means they will need to start by inviting many more than ten guests, and by confirming at least fourteen people personally (with reminder postcards and phone calls) at least twice as the event approaches, including once the day before the event. That is what it will take to produce ten people at their table on the day of the event.

Your projected fundraising numbers for the event should presume that no more than fifty percent of the guests will make a financial contribution that day. The other fifty percent may choose to come to a "real" Point of Entry after the event to learn more, to talk with someone else before making their gift or not to give at all. In other words, the event organizers need to be counting on only half the people giving.

Again, for many of the guests who have been to Points of Entry and subsequently well-cultivated according to the Raising More Money Model, this event will be the first time they have been asked to give. For long-time supporters of the organization, the event will be a reaffirmation of their wise investment and they may choose to give again. For brand-new people, the Free One-Hour Ask Event will serve as their Point of Entry, and they will most likely need more time or involvement before they choose to give.

On the morning of the event, the Table Captains arrive early to greet their guests. The guests arrive, somewhat confused, wondering what this is all about, looking for the coffee. Though they have been told this is a one-hour event, no one believes it. People are assuming they will need to slip out a little early, write a check and get back to their workplace.

Instead, you wake them up, dazzle them, inspire them and then ask for their money, all within sixty minutes. In this world of instant gratification, given the rate at which things zip by, you have got to be able to make an indelible impact on people in sixty minutes or less. They need to see right away that this organization is different. From the moment they get out of their cars at the front of the hotel or restaurant, you have to shake up their reality by having someone there to greet them—real people who are a part of your organization, staff, students, volunteers, whoever is appropriate.

Remember, this event is part of your cycle of building lifelong donors. You are not looking for one-time donors here. If the event provides an unforgettable introduction to your organization's fine work, you will have gotten the job done.

THE FLOW OF THE EVENT

To illustrate the entire event process, I'll use an example from Zion Preparatory Academy, the extraordinary inner-city private school referred to earlier where this event has been done several years in a row, reaping great rewards.

(Note: Do not be dissuaded from trying this type of event if your organization does not have "cute kids" to show off and talk about. The format of this event can easily be modified for all types of organizations, including national policy organizations, arts organizations, professional associations, etc.)

As you get out of your car at the front door of the hotel, there to greet you are two elementary school students, holding hands. Dressed in their plaid uniforms, bright-eyed and freshly scrubbed, they greet you with big smiles. "Good morning, welcome to the breakfast event; thank you for coming; just go right this way." You enter the hotel to find another pair of students who shake your hand, welcome you, and guide you up the escalator to the mezzanine level where the ballroom is located.

As you ride up the escalator wondering what this is all about, you hear music. You can't see the ballroom yet, but you can hear the voices of a children's choir, accompanied by an organ, singing rousing songs that put you in the mood. You arrive at the ballroom level, find your nametag with your table number on a table in the lobby, and hurry in to find your table. You greet your friend the Table Captain and find your place.

At the stroke of 7:30 a.m., the event begins, as scheduled. While generally only sixty percent of the guests are on time, this event is orchestrated like a space shuttle launch and every minute counts. Although people are still arriving, you start on time with the perfunctory welcome to everyone by the board chair who also thanks the board members, the Table Captains and other visiting dignitaries. To add another taste of your mission, there is an invocation delivered by a pastor and child, a short Emotional Hook that reminds people of the agenda at hand.

Then the board chair tells everyone, "Enjoy your breakfast. We'll be back to start the program in about ten minutes." You must give people time to be social with the other people at their table. Otherwise, people will feel they are being rude. Yet given that every single one of our sixty minutes counts, you want to use this ten minutes of "down time" to forward the crescendo you are building.

As you are eating your breakfast (a cold breakfast with the tables already set with lots of food, including hot coffee), talking to the person next to you, you feel a tap on your shoulder. You turn around to see a child holding a basket of apples, offering you one. "Thank you for coming today, would you like an apple?" It happens so fast that, for most of the guests, the impact is almost subliminal, yet people do remember: This is a real child who goes to this school. This is a child who could benefit if I give money today.

Also, as you are eating your breakfast, you notice the drawings in the center of the tables or inserted in the programs. On half-sized paper are crayon drawings of what each child wants to be when he or she grows up. They have written below the drawings, in their own words, "I want to be a teacher, a scientist, a pilot, etc." These "center-pieces" become conversation pieces at the tables and people take them home as mementoes of the event.

The program begins again. Similar to the Point of Entry Event, which more than half these guests have already attended, the Vision-ary Leader speaks in a very inspiring way for seven minutes about the mission, the philosophy, and why the work of this school is so essen-tial. The Visionary Leader then introduces the video, a seven-minute virtual tour of the school, including testimonials from students, par-ents and teachers. The video moves people to tears several times as it drives home the message. The lights come back on, gradually.

Next on the agenda are testimonials that begin with the school choir singing two songs, quickly and adorably. There is nothing quite like the sound of kids' voices singing to inspire people. Then, while they are still assembled on the risers on the stage, children in the choir are interviewed by a well-know local media personality. Hold-ing her microphone to their faces one by one, she asks: "Why do you like going to this school?"

"Oh, my teacher, I love my teacher."

"The hugs I get in the morning."

"The food; I love the food."

Next question: "What's your favorite subject?"

"Math."

"Science."

"Math."

"Math."

"Reading."

And finally: "What do you want to be when you grow up?" This is where the audience melts. Here are little children, belting out in their loudest voices, not what they want to be, but what they are going to be. The children start saying the kinds of things they had written on their drawings at the tables:

"I'm going to be a scientist."

"A teacher."

"An engineer."

In that moment, even if you have never heard of this school before and have only come because your friend the Table Captain invited you, you are moved. You can see that whether or not they ever become a pilot or teacher, each child has a vision and a dream for their lives. Given the statistics you heard during the presentation and the video, you know it is not a foregone conclusion that each of these children will grow up with the likelihood of a bright future. You can see and feel that something is happening at this school that is changing lives. If you are ever going to make a contribution to a program like this, this school definitely seems to know what it is doing. It would be a good investment.

Next on the program (now fifty minutes into the hour) is the "pitch" person—perhaps a chairman of the board of a major corporation, someone with a lot of credibility, or someone closely connected to the mission of the organization, even a family member. Knowing that by now the audience is well warmed-up, he does not need to convince people to give. In fact, any more convincing would cause overripe fruit. His job is to ask in a very straightforward manner.

When we go to an Ask Event, we know what is coming. As this person gets up to do the pitch, people are already thinking about how much they can give. "What will my spouse or partner say?" "How much room is on my credit card?" At this point, each of us tends to get very focused on ourselves and to stop paying attention to the speaker. That is why smart "pitch" people know that, at this point in the event, their job is to just walk people through the pledge card step by step.

He introduces himself, saying he is part of the fundraising board of the school. "I love this school. In the last hour, you have met our students, you have seen our programs. My job today is to ask for your support. I'd like to ask the Table Captains to pass out the pledge cards now." Note that the pledge cards were not waiting at your place when you arrived for breakfast. If they had been, many people would have filled them out before they had absorbed the program and some might have left early.

He pauses while the pledge cards are distributed. "Now we know that most of you had no idea what we were going to ask you for today. You came because your friend invited you. And others of you are already familiar with the school. Perhaps you've taken one of our tours. When we looked at what we wanted to ask you for today, we decided to ask for what we really need. We have approximately six hundred students at the school. Parents and family members work hard to pay the tuition. Yet there is still a gap. Our shortfall each year is $600,000.

"Today we're asking those of you who can make a contribution of $1,000 a year to Sponsor a Student by pledging to do that for the next five years. It will provide stability for our students and the school administration to know that you'll be doing that for five years. One thousand dollars is $83 a month. Please check off the first box on the pledge card if you can do that.

"This is not a scholarship program. Your money does not go directly to a particular student. As much as anything, these categories are just gimmicks to have people feel connected to our school. All of the money raised today supports the general operations of the school, to enable the staff to continue doing the outstanding work you've seen here today."

He pauses between each category to give people a chance to fill out the card. Then he says, "Some of you are capable of giving more. You may have a corporation, a family foundation, or just the capacity to give at a larger level. We have twenty-five students in each classroom. We'd like you to consider giving $25,000 a year for the next five years to Sponsor a Classroom of students. If you can do that, check the second box.

"Now, some of you who can do that may want to become involved with a particular classroom of kids, and stay with them over the next five years. You may want to have your staff or family come out and put on parties or do special projects. That's great. Others of you may not want to get involved that directly. You're happy just to give the money to support this classroom. That's fine, too.

"Moving down to the next box on your form: Some of you don't like giving to operating needs. You'd rather give to an endowment fund. If you give a gift of $20,000, or $5,000 a year for four years, we'll put that money in an investment account. We figure, conservatively, it will earn 5% interest. That annual interest equals $1,000 a year (the same amount as the first category, the Sponsor a Student category). You would be Endowing a (place for a) Student forever."

He pauses to catch his breath and repeats, "We know most of you did not know how much we were going to ask you for today. You came because your friend invited you. We started by asking you to give in these larger categories. I hope that many of you have chosen to do that.

"Now, I'd like to ask those of you who have not yet given to tell us how much you'd like to give and for how long. The fourth box on the pledge card lets you do that. Whatever you can give, we truly appreciate." (Note: This is the fill-in-the-blanks category, letting the donor determine their own giving level and number of years.)

"Finally, perhaps you want more information, would like to take a tour of the school, etc. Please check the last box, the one that says: 'Please contact me, I have other thoughts to share.' Thank you again for your support for our children." He pauses to give the guests several minutes to fill out the form. Then he turns the program over to the emcee to wrap it up.

Sixty minutes and the event is over. People are inspired. They linger to talk to friends. A tape of the children singing is playing in the background.

In the space of that hour, more than $1 million has been raised, including pledges. People have not felt pressured. The people who gave are glad they did. The people who did not give do not feel uncomfortable about not giving.

About half the guests had already been to a Point of Entry tour at the school. They had received Follow-Up Calls and many had become involved. For the other half of the guests, this event was their Point of Entry Event. After all, it contained the Facts, the Emotional Hook, and a mechanism for Capturing the Names. Some guests jumped right in and gave anyway. Others were just absorbing the first round of information.

SUMMARY

Let's review the major points about the Free One-Hour Ask Event. First, it needs to be free. For the event just described, had there been any admission charge for the breakfast, the event would not have been nearly as successful. In the new reality, the free event allows people the freedom to choose, and as a result they will give more generously.

Second, remember the two key ingredients of any Ask: Units of Service and the multiple-year pledges. Looking at the event for the school, consider this: What if, after all that outstanding work had been done to educate and inspire people, instead of asking for specific amounts, the "pitch" person had said, "Please give generously. We ask you to give from the bottom of your hearts."

What does that mean? In this day and age, people need specific categories. Otherwise, those who are highly capable of giving might not know that it is alright to make a larger gift at this event. And those with less giving capacity might feel that their smaller gift might be insignificant. Without specific giving categories, you will have put all that work into an event that could have brought in more than a million dollars and you may find yourself settling for $20,000 or $30,000.

Likewise, why not ask for a multiple-year pledge? These people have gone to all the trouble to get there. They have sat through your outstanding program. They were genuinely moved to contribute. Why not seize the moment and ask them to commit to give for several years?

People know they do not have to make a multiple-year pledge. You have given them the option to give one year at a time. Therefore, those who do choose to give at the multiple-year levels are telling you something with their pledge. They are telling you that they want to be more closely connected to your organization. They are "with you" on your mission. They want you to stay in touch with them.

Once you ask for multiple-year pledges for your annual operating needs, you will not regret it. If anything, as the fifth year rolls around, you will wish you had asked people to give for ten years, not five.

Sample Pledge Card Wording

(ORGANIZATION NAME) CAN COUNT ON MY SUPPORT!

Date _____

Name _____

Organization _____

Address _____

City _____ State _____ Zip _____

Day Phone _____ Evening Phone _____

Email Address _____

I would like to become a founding member of the Dream Builder Society:

___ Sponser a Student: $1,000 per year for 5 years

___ Sponser a Classroom of students: $25,000 per year for 5 years

___ Endow a place for a Student: $20,000 (to be paid over_____ years)

I would like to contribute in other ways:

___ Contribute $_____ for _____ years

___ Please contact me. I have other thoughts to share.

PAYMENT:

___ My check is enclosed, made payable to:

___ Please charge my Visa/MC#_____Exp._____

___ Please contact me about paying my pledge with stock.

___ My company will match my gift.

We will bill you every November for your annual pledge unless you request otherwise:

_____

CHAPTER 17

FREE FEEL-GOOD CULTIVATION EVENTS

The fourth type of event is the Free Feel-Good Cultivation Event, also known as a Point of Re-Entry Event. These events are not optional in the Raising More Money Model. They are essential to deepening your relationships with your donors.

Many of the events you now have that are free to guests to attend, such as donor or volunteer recognition events, awards ceremonies or graduations, will fall into this category. These events are aimed at prior donors as a "reward" for their loyal support. They powerfully reconnect the donor to the mission of the organization and reinforce their original decision to give. Just as with a Point of Entry, the Point of Re-Entry or Free Feel-Good Cultivation Event gives people the Facts 101, the Emotional Hook and a permission-based method for Capturing the Names. Donors leave feeling good, saying to themselves: "I'm glad I give money there. I will keep doing that. Maybe I could give more."

No one is asked to give at these events. These are strictly reward and reinforcement events. It is wise to encourage prior donors to invite "new" people to these events. For the new people, the event will be a Point of Entry. Just be sure to do the rigorous follow-up work we have described.

Free Feel-Good Cultivation Events take on many forms. Most obvious is the traditional recognition event such as the awards dinner or the more informal picnics, barbecues or dinner parties in private homes. In a second category are the informal, yet invitation-only, in-house program related events such as a special night for donors to serve soup in your soup kitchen or a special pre-graduation reception for Multiple-Year Society Donors. In the third category are the formal or informal briefings or updates with a celebrity scientist or artist on their newest work or discovery.

Let's look at some examples.

EXAMPLE 1:
TRADITIONAL RECOGNITION DINNER

The donor recognition dinner is the classic example of a highly effective Free Feel-Good Cultivation Event. This event may be aimed at donors at a certain dollar level who are invited to a special home or boat or garden where they are thanked, honored and reconnected to the facts and emotional impact of your work. Or it may be a larger event to thank and recognize all of your donors.

Let the guests know in advance there will be a short program. Begin with a welcome and thank-you from one of your key board members. Plaques or something more personal, such as a framed child's drawing, may be presented to each donor. Then be sure you include at least one live testimonial from a client, family member, volunteer or staff member—and make it good.

Next, the Visionary Leader briefs the donors on the state of the organization for no more than five minutes, telling them how far you have come thanks to their help. Then the leader paints the picture of the organization's future, the next phase of the dream, the next level of needs. This can border on a "soft" Ask. "We're looking forward to building our own building in the next three years. You'll be hearing more about that as the time comes closer."

The Visionary Leader can even mention a Challenge Gift that has been received or, better yet, announce the challenge now to these donors as insiders. If the donors to the Challenge Gift Fund are present, have them say what inspired them to contribute in this way. It will help launch the next phase of the campaign and encourage people to increase their gifts. It is fine to have the Visionary Leader or board member say, "We are still looking for other gifts to be added to our Challenge Fund." That way no one will feel left out.

Notice all this is strictly informational. No one is being asked. After all, these donors are your inside family. If you were part of the family, you would not want to hear about this big news indirectly. You would want to be among the first to know. Perhaps you would have an opinion about it.

With your loyal donors, the issue is not when and how to ask them for money, but making sure you don't offend them by inadvertently overlooking them in some way. This is where your ongoing follow-up pays off. Someone knows those donors well enough to be able to anticipate how the program at your Free Feel-Good Cultivation Event will sound to them. It is as if you could do a dress rehearsal of the event and know how each person in the audience will receive and interpret the information.

The entire program for this event should last no more than thirty minutes. Then give people plenty of time to mix and mingle. The networking effect of these events is magical. Be sure the crowd is interspersed with board and staff members who can give you feedback on each guest the next day. Since this is a Point of Re-Entry Event, you will be starting the cycle with them again by making Follow-Up Calls.

EXAMPLE 2:
IN-HOUSE PROGRAM-RELATED EVENT

Another type of Free Feel-Good Cultivation Event is a regularly scheduled program-related event with your constituents or clients, to which donors are invited. One hospital neonatal intensive care unit invites donors to the annual reunion of parents and their (now grown) premature babies. This includes a special reception for donors with a fireside chat update from the head physician in the pediatrics unit and the head of the hospital. As mentioned earlier, other regularly scheduled in-house program events that can be easily converted to Free Feel-Good Cultivation Events are graduation ceremonies preceded by a special reception with the principal and board, and performing arts rehearsals with backstage chats with the actors or director.

EXAMPLE 3:
THE ISSUE-ORIENTED FORUM

A third example of a Free Feel-Good Cultivation or Point of Re-Entry Event is a private, issue-oriented forum with a sought-after speaker. This works well for policy, research or national organizations and can be taken on the road. Just be sure to include enough emotion in the testimonials and the impassioned dream of the Visionary Leader. Otherwise you will have an intellectual evening, which is not sufficient to re-connect guests and donors to your mission.

PLANNING THESE POINTS OF
RE-ENTRY STRATEGICALLY

I recommend a minimum of one Free Feel-Good Cultivation Event per year, targeted to your Multiple Year Giving Society members. In addition, it is a good idea to have a second event for all of your donors.

As for best times of year to hold these events, they are most often scheduled to occur about three months after your Ask Events or else to coincide with natural program events such as arts performances and graduations.

Next, let's look at the glue that pulls the system together: Follow-Up.

CHAPTER 18

FOLLOW-UP AND BEYOND

As you have seen throughout this book, the Point of Entry is only that: a Point of *Entry*—the first step in a potential lifelong donor's relationship with your organization. Without impeccable follow-up and cultivation you will have done nothing more than burdened your organization with a new series of labor-intensive events.

If, on the other hand, you take each step of the model as seriously as you take the Point of Entry, you will leave a lasting legacy of lifelong, mission-based donors for your organization.

Consider this example: Imagine yourself as one of the guests at your organization's Point of Entry Event—a tour, a reception, a box-lunch informational meeting. You attended one event and you were impressed. You could see that this organization is right on the mark.

Now what? They didn't ask you for money. They sent you home with some materials. You take a minute to read them. How interesting. There is an easy-to-read Wish List of all kinds of things they need. There are little items like toothbrushes, shampoo, pots and pans, help in the office once a week. And there are some medium-sized items like old computers, carpeting for the youth room, a van, math tutors. The list goes all the way up to the really big stuff: a new gymnasium, an underwriter for their international conference, a new office building, a properly staffed reading program.

You see that you could actually contribute some of the things on that list, but you are too busy to pick up the phone and call them or you might not want to appear that "forward." You put away the

Wish List and go on to the next activity in your day.

Two days later, you get a phone call from that nice staff person you met at the tour or lunch meeting. She is thanking you for taking your time to come and asking for your input. "What did you think of our program?" You tell her in a reserved way how impressed you were. You mention that the intercultural studies program was especially appealing. At some point, she asks: "Is there any way you could see yourself becoming involved?"

You may be thinking about underwriting that international conference. After all, it links to many other interests of yours, yet you don't want to lead off with something so big. "I notice you need some old computers," you respond. "I could help you with that."

She is very appreciative and tells you immediately how much they are needed and for which program. The demand has increased so much that the computer lab is now open every evening and there are still people who can't get the computer time they need. My goodness, you are thinking, my old computers could really make a difference. We've upgraded our system at the office and those old ones are actually in the way. I'd be a real hero if I found a good cause to donate them to.

"Would it help if we came to pick them up?" she offers. "I know how happy it will make the people in the computer lab to have them before the new round of classes starts." Next thing you know, they have picked up the computers and you are getting a call inviting you to come back and see the expanded computer program in action one evening when it is in full swing.

"Feel free to invite anyone else you'd like," offers that same warm, efficient staff person.

You arrive with your husband and two work colleagues just to check it out on your way to dinner. You are dazzled. Those old computers that had been cluttering the back room at the office are now front and center, with eager, curious children and their parents clicking away. The head of the computer program, a brainy-looking fellow, happens to be there in the midst of all the action. He can't thank you enough.

Of course, as part of the evening's show-and-tell of the computer center, your low-key guide points out the students from the intercultural program, communicating with their international "e-pals". "It's just a start," she says, "they're always hungry for more real connections with other cultures." Your friends leave their cards to come back and attend the full Point of Entry Event, and you go off to dinner. Everyone is feeling good, and you are looking like the person of the hour. For your friends, this was a mini-Point of Entry Event. For you, it was a validation that you picked a winner.

The next week, the same nice staff person calls back to thank you for coming out again and for bringing those friends. "What did they think of it?" she asks. "Do you think they'd have any interest in getting involved? Would it be all right with you if I give them a call? Is there any more you would like in the way of information or involvement?"

And so it goes. A one-time visit to a Point of Entry Event and an effective Follow-Up Call lead to more and more.

A few points to consider:

- Are you making your needs known to first-time, potential contributors?

- Do you have a Wish List with a wide array of items you'd really love to have? Could you link each item to a staff person or department that would be thrilled to receive them?

- If someone chooses to get involved on a volunteer basis, are you prepared to take care of them to ensure a super-positive experience?

- What if they identify an area of interest that you've never thought of? Are you flexible enough to think it through together?

Today's potential donors want to get involved in meaningful ways. They want to call the shots. They want to control the pace of their relationship with you. They are prepared to be loyal. They are always testing to be sure you really need them. They appreciate an honest answer more than an obvious, polite response. They are looking for the perfect blend of their talents and resources with your needs. And so are you!

The Follow-Up Call is your ticket to customizing the ideal type of involvement for that donor. It is essential to building a self-sustaining, individual-giving program in the new fundraising reality.

Please take the time to think through the follow-up.

First, who is the best person to be accountable for insuring that every single Point of Entry guest receives that call within one week? Do not give this responsibility to someone who is already overloaded with work, unless of course you offload some of that work and free them up to do this job.

Ideally this will be the person accountable for the overall implementation of the Raising More Money Model within your organization. This person must attend each Point of Entry Event, since you will only want Follow-Up Calls made by a person who the guest met at the event. The caller needs to be someone who has a direct line to the head of the organization, someone with maturity, "people skills," and outstanding organizational skills. It needs to be someone who can screen the many good ideas people will have for you, and someone with the authority to act on them or to pull together the decision makers who can act quickly. A donor or potential donor with a hot idea expects and deserves immediate attention. That way, each donor will be shepherded through the process by the same friendly person who has been with them all along. This continuity matters to people. Take the time to assign this job to the right person.

If you decide to have more than one person responsible for follow-up, be sure they share a computer database and update each other regularly. You might want to assign each of them to be the Donor Service Representative for their own group of donors so that those donors feel they have their own contact person.

Do not overlook senior level staff for this position. Consider what parts of their job may have become rote and perfunctory, yet would be considered exciting and challenging to someone else. Also consider delegating to volunteers. One example from my own experience at the school was a woman who, after attending a Point of Entry Event, mentioned in the Follow-Up Call that she liked to write. She subsequently became our volunteer grant writer, writing and sending out as many as five grant requests a week, while working at a high-powered full-time job. She used this experience—and the financial success of the grants she wrote—to build her resume. She now is the executive director of a well-respected United Way, a position she might never have considered otherwise.

In some smaller organizations, the executive director takes on this accountability. Often they tell us in our workshops, "This is what I am really supposed to be doing. And besides, I am out there anyway making these contacts." While this may seem time-consuming for a busy executive director, by designing and implementing the process themselves, these executive directors then know the job description well enough to hire a development director down the road who will be successful at the job. All too often we see the high turnover in directors of development because an executive director did not know what the job really entailed and therefore was ill-prepared to manage the development director to produce the needed results.

Conversely, there may be another shining star, lower down in the organizational hierarchy, who everyone has been noticing for their enthusiasm and organizational abilities.

Whoever takes this on has to want to do it. Most traditional director of development positions in small- to medium-sized (and even many large) organizations are consumed with grant writing, special events and direct mailings. This job description is completely different from that. Please do not inform someone after the fact that they are now responsible for implementing the Raising More Money Model within your organization. They will be resentful and leave. Far better to find the person who wants to do this, get them the proper training and support and empower them to be successful.

Even in the best of circumstances, shifting the underlying context for fundraising within a nonprofit organization can be a daunting task. Try to stack the deck for the lead person to be successful. Then back that person up with a small, outstanding team. As the program grows and more and more people come through your Point of Entry or Point of Entry Conversion Events, this person will need significant help. Giving each potential donor the personalized time and attention they need along the Cultivation Superhighway will be well worth the effort.

INVOLVING OTHERS IN THE
POINT OF ENTRY PROCESS

CHAPTER 19

INVOLVING YOUR BOARD

There is no question that the support and involvement of board members is essential to the success of your Point of Entry program. While you certainly do not need the buy-in of each and every board member, your program will be much more successful with a core group of board members who understand and endorse this approach.

In other words, please do not use lack of one hundred percent board support for the Raising More Money Model as an excuse for postponing getting started. As with any change, people will warm up to it at their own pace. Welcome the board members who are "early adopters" of this new approach and be patient with the others.

I recommend you have the buy-in of at least two credible and well-respected board members before you begin your program in earnest. If you already have a development committee in place, you may have two or more supporters there. If your development committee has been less than effective, this may be the ideal time to reconfigure your committees and let some of the former members go, replacing them with a small group that is enthusiastic about this model. Ironically, the power of your Point of Entry Events will attract new, passionate members to your board. No doubt some of them will make ideal candidates for your new committee.

The easiest way to achieve that buy-in from your board is to— guess what? Invite them to a Point of Entry Event. Have it be the real thing, not a staged mock-up. Schedule it at a separate time from your regular board meeting. Let the board know that these one-hour Points of Entry are something new you would like to start offering on a regular basis to help spread the word about your work in the community. While you know that they are already familiar with the work of the organization, you would greatly appreciate their advice and critique of one of the first Point of Entry Events before you open them up to the public. Tell them enough about the program elements to entice them. Encourage them to bring a friend or family member who may not know much about your organization. Promise them that it will only last one hour and that no one will be asked to give money there. Give them two dates to choose from.

Then, make it great! Put on your inspiring and concise one hour Point of Entry Event and watch their reaction. Even if they do not bring others with them, they will notice the favorable response of other newcomers. They will see that the event is not at all threatening or overbearing. They may tell you that it reconnected them with the reason they first got involved with your organization.

As with all of your future Point of Entry guests, make a one-on-one Follow-Up Call to your board members after the event to gather their feedback. Follow our standard five-step Follow-Up Call format. Take good notes and do everything that you can to incorporate the feedback they give you. After all, this is your board. They are your most treasured advocates in the community. Whatever feedback they are giving you is important and is based in their support for the organization. If they are going to feel comfortable inviting people to Points of Entry, they have got to know that their concerns have been heard and, ideally, addressed.

These Follow-Up Calls with board members after they attend this first "demo" Point of Entry may also help you to identify candidates for your Raising More Money implementation team or committee. Chapter 27 contains a description of the planning retreat you will want to have with this committee or team.

For all of the other board members who choose not to become directly involved, there are many ways for them to participate indirectly. Here are some suggestions for turning your Points of Entry into a well-oiled system at the board level:

1. Schedule your Point of Entry Events for the next year and show the calendar to your board. Tell them you would like each of them to consider hosting one of these events. Define what you mean by hosting: Board members are not expected to fill the room with their friends, but rather to attend themselves and greet the other guests on behalf of the board. Of course if they would like to invite others, they are welcome to do so.

2. Invite board members to consider hosting a separate Point of Entry in a Box at a location of their choice; for example, their office or home or even a private Point of Entry at your locations. While there is certainly no expectation or requirement that they do this, for some board members this may be more convenient and feel more personal than inviting friends to an introductory event that is open to the public.

3. Make up business cards for the organization with the dates and locations of all upcoming Points of Entry. Have these cards available at all board meetings for board members to take and keep with them throughout the month, making it easier for them to invite others. Be sure to remind them to have their guests RSVP. (See sample of card at the end of this chapter.)

   While some of their friends might choose to come to the event hosted by their friend the board member, others may need alternative dates. Eventually board members will come to trust that their friends will be "safe" at a Point of Entry, even if they themselves are not there to accompany them.

4. At each board meeting, have board members report about their guests' reactions to the Point of Entry, as well as their own reaction, if they were able to accompany their guest. You will be delighted by the good things they say. This will reassure and encourage other board members to begin inviting.

5. Keep a list of Point of Entry guests and circulate it at monthly board meetings. Board members will be curious. They will notice names of friends and acquaintances and may naturally be able to follow up informally as they see these people in their daily lives. These board conversations with recent Point of Entry guests count as contacts on the Cultivation Superhighway and will help to ripen the fruit.

| Point of Entry Guest Tracking Sheet | | |
Date of Point of Entry	Name of Guest	Invited By
1		
2		
3		
4		
5		
6		
7		
8		
9		
10		
11		
12		
13		
14		
15		

6. Be sure to include the name of the person who invited each guest on the list of Point of Entry guests. Board members will notice. Some may be mentally keeping score and, at a certain point, may feel they are ready to invite someone as well.

7. As part of your larger fundraising report to the board of money raised each month, highlight those new donors who attended Points of Entry. Give the board specific evidence that the program is working.

Finally, the most important thing to keep in mind as you interact with your board members regarding Points of Entry is the longer-term objective: building lifelong donors. And who better to become lifelong donors than these very board members? Regardless of their giving capacity or their personality styles, you want to treat your board members with the same appreciation and respect as you would treat any other volunteer or donor. Be generous in your thanks and appreciation of your board members, both publicly and privately, for their support.

SAMPLE: **POINT OF ENTRY REMINDER CARD**

Open House
N Street Village

Please call 202-939-2072 to reserve. Group size limited.

We invite you to tour N Street Village on the second Sunday and Wednesday of each month.

Enter the Eden House lobby at 1301 14th Street NW (14th and N Streets).

N Street Village is accessible from the Dupont Circle or McPherson Square Metro Stations. On-street parking is available. Paid parking is available at the Washington Plaza Hotel at 10 Thomas circle.

Open House 1998

Sunday, August 8, 2:00 pm
Wednesday, August 12, 12:00 pm
Sunday, September 13, 2:00 pm
Wednesday, September 16, 12:00 pm
Sunday, October 11, 2:00 pm
Wednesday, October 14, 12:00 pm
Sunday, November 8, 2:00 pm
Wednesday, November 11, 12:00 pm
Sunday, December 13, 2:00 pm
Wednesday, December 16, 12:00 pm

Allow 60 minutes for the program and tour.

(N Street Village, Washington DC)

CHAPTER 20

INVOLVING STAFF

Staff plays a key role in the success of your Point of Entry system.

We saw as we composed the Treasure Map that all roads led to the staff. The staff tends to be one group on the Treasure Map that talks to nearly every other group. When we looked at selecting testimonial speakers, we saw that staff members often have the best stories to share. The staff can supply you with a long list of items for your Wish List. Staff members may want to be Table Captains at your Free One-Hour Ask Event. If you are taking people on a tour of your offices, you will want to be sure the staff understands the purpose of these tours and what they are designed to produce in the long run for the organization. The staff can be invaluable in critiquing and refining the information you are presenting at your Point of Entry. I remember how much we modified what we said at our school Point of Entry Events after bringing teachers through the tours and asking them for feedback about how to present their classroom curriculum.

As such, you will want to make a special effort to secure staff buy-in early in the process and to keep your staff involved over time. While your fundraising efforts will ultimately benefit the whole staff, this may not be readily apparent to them at the outset. Put yourself in their place for a moment. They were not hired to do the fundraising. They were hired to run a program and, like you, they have specific objectives they must meet. In other words, fundraising is not their job. To put it bluntly, in the short run, you need them more than they need you.

When was the last time you spent a day (or even an hour) shadowing one of your organization's front-line staff members? It would probably give you a far greater appreciation of any resistance you may be encountering as you approach them to talk about your cherished Point of Entry Events. You will have to make sure that the self-interest of your staff is served by helping you.

For most staff, money is not the driver. It is knowing that their program is presented accurately to the public. Your artistic director most likely cringes at the thought of the business-minded development director having to describe the essence of their art. Same with your research scientists, gay-youth advocates or foster care workers. Their self-interest in helping you is to ensure that the story of their program is being told powerfully, protecting whatever information needs to be protected, while still conveying the need.

In fact, they are right. As a fund development person, you would probably cringe just as much at the thought of them explaining to some of their artists or scientists or fellow advocates or foster care workers just what it is that you do every day.

The smart thing, all the way around, would be to let the staff help you tell the story in the most powerful way. Beyond that, involve them only to the extent they request to be involved and let them go about getting their own jobs done. Appreciate them for the wonderful work they are doing. After all, without the staff you would not have a program to raise that money for.

Here is a suggested scenario for how you might involve your staff in the Point of Entry process.

1. Meet with your staff as a whole or in subgroups to explain the new Point of Entry program you will be starting to build lifelong donors. You may need to do a mini-training to show them the Raising More Money Model and invite their input.

2. Tell them the kinds of things the money you raise will be used for. Be as straight with them as possible, even if it means telling them that their program will probably not benefit directly from your efforts. They will appreciate your honesty.

3. Put on a special Point of Entry Event just for the staff and invite their critical feedback, ideally one-on-one afterwards. Let them tell you how they would like you to describe their program to visitors.

4. Get them talking about what keeps them working here, doing their work day-to-day. Notice whether or not their stories inspire you. This will be helpful as you design the Essential Story and how it relates to all the elements of your Emotional Hook.

5. Tell them clearly and honestly how your Point of Entry Events will affect them. If the events include a tour, you may be intruding on the staff's daily work as you bring visitors through. Will you want them to speak at the Point of Entry or to share stories from the front lines?

6. You might want to show them your Treasure Map, or, better yet, make a new one with them, to get them thinking of people to invite to the Point of Entry Events. This might be the perfect opportunity for them to finally invite their friends and family to come and see firsthand where they work. Remember, everyone is welcome at a Point of Entry Event. You never know who is on their Treasure Map.

7. Invite staff members to be part of your team. There may be that exceptional person who does not work in the fund development area who would love to be a part of the effort. Be sure to include them.

8. Invite the staff to attend all of your Point of Entry-related events, especially if you will be talking about their programs. This includes your annual Free Feel-Good Cultivation Event where a volunteer or client from their area may

be receiving an award. Encourage staff members to be Table Captains at your Free One-Hour Ask Event. While most staff members will not take you up on the offer, some may prove to be real assets to your team.

9. Give the staff regular feedback about the results of your individual giving program. Anecdotal comments from visitors about the caring, expert staff are always appreciated. Keep them updated on the results of the fundraising program. As much as possible, show tangible evidence of what the money has been used for.

Your underlying message to staff is that you value their work, and that you are their partner in spreading the word about their good work in the community. As such, you need one another.

CHAPTER 21

INVOLVING VOLUNTEERS

$\mathbf{W}$e have talked about the critical role that board members and staff will play in successfully implementing Points of Entry into your organization's culture. Volunteers are equally critical, especially when you recognize that every volunteer is a potential donor and every donor a potential volunteer.

INVITE THEM TO A SPECIAL POINT OF ENTRY

The easiest way to get your existing volunteers involved in the program is to invite them to their own special Point of Entry. Just as you did for your board and staff, hosting this special event tells lets them in on your new program early and tells them how special they are to you.

Next, just as you have done with your board and staff, you will want to plan a special Point of Entry just for your volunteers. This will help them trust the process and feel more comfortable inviting others. Do not assume, just because they have been volunteering with you for months or years and may be very familiar with your organization, that they know or trust what a Point of Entry would be like enough to have them invite their friends.

Ask one or two of your key volunteers to help you plan this first Point of Entry for your volunteers. If you have many subgroups of volunteers, you may need to have many of these initial Points of Entry. You may choose to involve the volunteers in putting on the

Point of Entry, or you may decide to treat them as special guests and not have them do any of the "work."

As part of the Emotional Hook at this special Point of Entry, be sure to have one or two volunteers give testimonials about the personal satisfaction and value they get from volunteering. This may be done in addition to the other testimonials you would normally include from staff or clients or family members.

FOLLOW UP AND INVOLVE

Then, just as you will do with every other person who comes to a Point of Entry, follow up by phone or in person with each volunteer within a week. Give them the opportunity to critique this event just as you did with your board members and staff. These conversations will be invaluable in helping you to see how people might like to become more involved, but only if you do not become defensive if they give you critical feedback.

Odds are, most will have advice for you about how you could have improved the Point of Entry. Some will focus on the way you spoke about the particular program they are involved with. For the most part, people will be incredibly proud of what you have done to pull this all together. And if you are honest in asking for their feedback and taking it to heart, they will begin to trust the process such that they would invite others to attend. After all, if they truly love the organization, they will want to share its good work with family and friends. What better way to introduce them than by having them attend a Point of Entry?

Based on what you learn in your Follow-Up Calls, tailor the next role for each volunteer accordingly. Most will be perfectly happy to keep going in the same role they have been in—as a tutor, a food bank volunteer or a friendly visitor to a shut-in elderly person. Some may discover new roles that would interest them more. If you are listening closely in the Follow-Up Calls, you may learn of other talents that they have to contribute, many of which you could put to good use right away. For example, some may offer to get more involved with fundraising! Perhaps they would like to be a Table Captain at your Ask Event or to serve on your team or committee for implementing the Raising More Money Model throughout your organization.

In other words, as you begin to treat your volunteers as you would treat any other donor or potential donor, you will learn more about their interests and passions and design roles and projects that might be a bit unconventional. The more you listen to your volunteers and let them drive the process, within reason, the sooner you will see the blurring of the lines between volunteers and donors. These same people who have been giving so generously of their time will begin giving you more money as well.

PROVIDE TRAINING

Most likely, out of following this process, you will discover or reconnect with many volunteers who are already, quite naturally, walking Points of Entry for your organization. You may want to give them some official "training" in doing your One-on-One Point of Entry and then deputize them to officially be out there in the world telling your organization's story.

While this may seem easy to staff who can effortlessly cite program facts and statistics along with plenty of emotional stories, for most volunteers this task can be daunting.

To review, the One-on-One Point of Entry covers the following points:

1. Who we are

2. Top three programs

3. Three little-known facts about our work

4. Why I work or volunteer here

5. I'll never forget the story about ...

6. Would you be interested in more information?

Make it easy on your volunteers by arming with them with all the information they will need. Make sure they can easily identify your top three programs. Give them simple, one-word descriptions. A faith-based program for single fathers listed its programs as: peer support, education and childcare.

Also, give your volunteers those three carefully crafted myth-buster facts and statistics about your work that leave people better informed and stirred up enough to take action, such as the incidence of a certain disease or problem right in their community, or the increased incidence of teenage pregnancy, smoking, divorce or air quality alerts.

Find out why they give their time to your organization. What is it about your group in particular that they value? If there is some personal reason they would be willing to mention, encourage them to do so.

As for the Essential Story, be sure each volunteer knows that classic story, or at least the general template for the story, that you feel best conveys the emotional impact of your work. If they have a story of their own they would prefer to use, ask them to tell it to you and be sure that it is truly inspiring.

Next, give them your schedule of upcoming Points of Entry, ideally on business cards with the name and address of the organization on the back, and encourage them to invite their friends to attend. In fact, you can print all of this up on a laminated business card that volunteers can carry with them. Some groups get so excited about this that they add a section on all of their regular business cards which lists their key programs, top three facts and dates of upcoming Points of Entry.

If you take the time to prepare your volunteers in this way, in a brief face-to-face meeting, either one-on-one or in a group of volunteers, they will likely realize that they feel comfortable talking about your organization and could do this on their own, with their friends, on an airplane, or at a party. Before you know it, you will have a greatly expanded team of goodwill ambassadors spreading the word and sending you guests for your Point of Entry Events.

LOOKING AHEAD

Now let's fast-forward to the impact of the Point of Entry system on your existing "volunteer" program.

Imagine, for example, that two years down the road you have had twenty-four Point of Entry Events, each with at least ten guests. That's two hundred and forty new people introduced to your organization. In addition, you have converted three of your other "fundraising events" to Point of Entry Conversion Events, which means you have been Capturing Names of those guests who are interested in learning more and you have been following up with them. Furthermore, you have put on one or two of the Free One-Hour Ask Events and you have at least fifty members of your Multiple-Year Giving Society who are coming to Free Feel-Good Cultivation Events every year.

In the course of your regular contact with these interested supporters or highly loyal donors, they will begin to offer other assistance with things that in the old-reality would have fallen on the fringes of the definition of a volunteer project, such as in-kind gifts or special projects. Yet, there may be no one in your organization equipped to deal creatively with each of these wonderful offers of support.

The first person who was hired to assist me after we got the Point of Entry system running smoothly at the school in Seattle was a wonderful woman who had the challenging job of interfacing between all of our new-found "volunteers" and the staff. If a volunteer/donor wanted to help us set up a new science or environmental program or a chess or reading program, we could not responsibly refer them to the teacher in that area. The teachers were already working double-time just to keep up with their teaching load. Yet we knew that the resources these new volunteers were offering would be invaluable to the quality of education the school was delivering.

What job title was I to give to this new staff person? Volunteer coordinator? Development assistant? Regardless of her title, having a person to fulfill this role is critical to the success of any new-reality individual giving program.

Furthermore, once we saw the deep commitment of time and money that these "volunteers" were willing to make, we realized that we needed to go back and begin treating our "regular" volunteers as if they had the same potential.

Over time, by customizing the entire Raising More Money Model to the needs of your own volunteers, you will have cultivated an ever-increasing group of loyal volunteers who will become life-long donors.

SPECIAL CONSIDERATIONS

CHAPTER 22

THE SEVEN-MINUTE VIDEO

If you are serious about adopting the Raising More Money Model, sooner of later you will need to have a video that showcases your organization's work, especially if you are planning to put on the Free One-Hour Ask Event. Once you have made this video, you may choose to use it at your Point of Entry Events, although *a video is not required for a Point of Entry.*

Having said that, there are many good reasons for using a video at your Points of Entry. Some organizations use video because they cannot show people their work firsthand due to confidentiality restrictions. In these cases the video is one component of the larger Point of Entry, which will include the Visionary Leader Talk and a testimonial speaker.

Other organizations develop a video that can be used as a stand-alone piece when staff members or volunteers take their Points of Entry "on the road" to meetings and group presentations at nearby or remote locations. They find the generic high quality of the video ensures that their message is delivered with consistency every time.

IT MUST EVOKE EMOTION

In either case—stand-alone or used as part of a larger program—the video has one main purpose: to evoke emotion. While you certainly want the video to educate people about your work, it is far more important that it inspire them and move them to tears. Do not expect your seven-minute video to cover each of your programs in detail. In fact, it may not cover each of them even briefly.

The challenge in producing a great video is to be able to synthesize your work down to its essence. Usually that means boiling it down to the impact of your organization on the lives of real people. After all, real people will be watching your video. Real people will be giving money to your organization. Remember: as individuals, we are emotional donors looking for rational reasons to justify our emotional decisions to give. If the guests at your events are not moved and inspired about your work, they will not be likely to give.

There are many other media that can be used effectively to educate and inspire people—PowerPoint presentations, slides, overhead transparencies, even audiotape. But when it comes to evoking emotion, nothing quite compares to a professionally made video.

The easiest example of this is television news. In the space of one to two minutes, a great news story gives you facts you can remember, the emotion of real human beings, action film footage and sound. Imagine, then, what you will be able to accomplish in seven minutes!

PRODUCING YOUR VIDEO

There are only two requirement of your video in the Raising More Money Model: it should be no longer than seven minutes and it must move people to tears three times.

Let's look at some ways you could accomplish that.

Probably the easiest and least expensive method is to edit some other video footage that has already been made about your organization. If you are fortunate to have had a television story done on your organization, odds are at least part of it captured the essence of your work. Perhaps they interviewed one of your staff members, volunteers or a consumer of your services. Usually, they will have focused on some aspect of your programming that represents one of the core aspects of your mission. You could, for example, use only the testimonial or interview footage and splice it together with your own video material that speaks to your larger mission. Or you could add in two other testimonials or stories about other programs you offer, or other sites of your work.

Perhaps your organization is part of a larger national organization or network of organizations that address a particular issue. Rather than going to the expense of making your own video, use all or parts of what already exists. Often the national office will have produced an excellent video, using generic examples, suitable for customizing to your region. In that case, decide which elements you want to showcase locally and have your video producer edit the national footage right into your locally produced video.

In our classes, we often recommend that the headquarters of national organizations catalog all their video footage so that local chapters can select the types of testimonials that best meet their needs, topically and demographically. They can pick and choose just what they need, saving costly duplication across chapters. In the case of a national health organization, for example, they could have cataloged and indexed video footage of testimonials from patients, doctors and family members of varying ages and ethnic backgrounds.

Whether you will be using existing footage or starting from scratch, producing a video will force you to figure out how to tell your complicated story in a succinct, emotional fashion. This can be a significant challenge.

I strongly recommend you engage a professional video producer, someone who has a track record of making this type of video. Take the time to find the right person. Most nonprofit organizations have someone associated with them who can help get a video made. Perhaps it is a person in the training department of a local corporation, a friend in the TV newsroom or a student at a local college. Finding a person to donate their services to produce a video may not be that difficult. The challenge is to find someone who can make this particular type of video.

Production Costs

Think twice before you accept a generous offer for donated video production. Often it comes with strings attached—by a volunteer, board member, or friend of a friend. Once you have accepted their offer, it becomes difficult to critique their work or request the number of edits that may be necessary to get what you want. All too often, we find groups who end up with a video that is only seventy-five percent of what they wanted, because it was too difficult to deal straight-forwardly with the pro bono video producer.

The cleanest way to get the video you want is to pay an expert to produce it for you. Current costs, depending on where you are located, range from $1,000 to $1,500 per finished minute. That means you should expect to pay as much as $10,000 for the final product.

Before you discard the notion of paying a professional to do the job, consider the many sources of funding available to you. First and most likely, you could apply for a grant from a local foundation or corporation—ideally one that already knows and appreciates your work. Make your case for the long-term value of having a top-quality video. In your proposal, explain why it is difficult to showcase your work firsthand (if it is) or why you feel the video is needed at your Ask Event.

Next, consider asking one donor to fund the cost of producing your video. One organization that participated in our workshop went to a grateful parent of a child whose life had been turned around by their fine work. The donor was delighted to fund the video, saying that they would do whatever they could to help spread the word so that other parents would not have to suffer. The organization gave credit to the donor at the end of the video—and it just happened to work out so that the donor's child's testimonial worked perfectly into the script!

Finally, do not overlook the possibility of paying for the video out of your budget. When you think of the hundreds of times it will be used, your investment will be quickly amortized. Many groups pay for the production costs from their own budgets and then have copies of their video donated by a corporation or individual donor. These copies are given to everyone who attends their Ask Event, or people who become founding members of their Multiple-Year Giving Society or even to people who were unable to attend the event. For the nominal duplication cost, your message can be widely disseminated and yield great results. While they may not read a book or even a brochure, most people will watch a video if it is given to them.

What to Include

Given the complex array of programs and services your organization offers, do not surrender the strategic decisions about video content to the producer. While their outsider perspective will be invaluable in making sense of your work to "real" people, it is your responsibility to make sure that they see and understand enough of what you do so that they have the full picture before they decide what to include and how to spin it.

Think of your standard litany of programs—the one you can recite in your sleep, the list you tell people whenever they ask what your organization does. Odds are that list is overkill for most people when recited verbally. Not only is it full of insider shorthand and jargon, but it would take too long to cover each of those programs even if everyone understood your language. Your job is to find the one umbrella theme or topic that includes all of your programs. Odds are, this will be—of all things—your mission. After all, you wouldn't be offering this diverse range of programs and services if they didn't somehow fit naturally under that umbrella called your mission.

I recommend that the heart and soul of your video be your mission. Have someone—ideally the Visionary Leader or one of the beneficiaries of your service—say that mission out loud in the video. Then relate each program to it.

Choose no more than three programs to showcase in your video. Find a way to link them to your mission and to each other. For each program, tell a few facts and have a testimonial speaker share how their life has changed, thanks to that program. Thread them together with a narrator or main voice (often one of your own staff or board). Another way to accomplish this is by having the narrator ask the same questions of each testimonial speaker. Questions like: "What was your life like before you learned about this organization?" "How did you hear about it?" "What is your life like now?" "What would you like others to know about this organization?"

Consider the elements of your Emotional Hook as you prepare the video. For example, if nostalgia is part of what moves people about your organization, you might interview your testimonial speakers about their favorite memories of camp, a former counselor or teacher. Think of what hooks you! It may not be as complicated as you'd expect.

Beyond the images and the voices, the music you choose can make all the difference. Recently I previewed a video for a group in one of our workshops. The footage was spectacular. Close-up action shots of the program participants deeply engaged in their work, stellar testimonials, yet the music was choppy and annoying. By simply substituting warmer, richer music, the same footage evoked far more emotion—which ultimately led to larger gifts. This is another reason to work with a professional. They know the range of musical backgrounds available. They should be able to offer you several selections to choose from.

TEST IT OUT

Finally, once you have refined the video to the point that you are satisfied with it, show it to several people who will tell you the truth. Odds are, it will need to be more emotional. Or perhaps people will tell you that it needs more factual content. While it may have moved them to tears, they still may not understand what your organization does or how some of the programs you offer fit together.

Two of my favorite videos were made very simply and on relatively low budgets. The first, put together by an organ donor organization, was a series of simple ten-second testimonials from organ donor recipients: "My life began again on May 10, 1993," spoken by a woman holding her baby, or the man on the golf course saying: "I got my new life on July 7, 1996." There were about twelve of these people who quickly each said the date they got their new lease on life thanks to a new organ that had been donated. The video also included a couple of people who were obviously quite debilitated, saying that every day they pray their phone would ring to hear the news that someone had donated the vital organ they needed.

All the while, in the background, was simple, moving music. The video was about five minutes long, interspersed will still shots of facts: "X number of people received organ transplants last year. X number died because there was no organ available. You could make the difference. Sign up to be an organ donor today."

The last testimonial was a man holding his baby and saying, "Every day of my life since March 22, 1997, has been a gift. I thank the Organ Donor Program for the gift of my life every single morning."

Because they were statewide agencies, they used the video at their Ask Events around the state, as well as at subsequent Point of Entry Events.

Another outstanding video was produced by a school for children with learning disabilities. It started with shots in the classroom of teachers and students deeply engaged in learning, then shifted to short clips of parents and children, one at a time, looking straight into the camera, saying thank you to a particular teacher who had changed their life or the life of their child. Great music, clean footage, no huge budget, less than seven minutes. A great investment.

Consider this example as another effective use of video: One family service organization sent copies of their video with a bag of microwave popcorn and a letter to everyone who was unable to attend their Ask Event. The letter invited them to sit down with their family—popcorn included—and watch the video together. It included two or three questions they might want to ask after viewing it. The letter ended by saying the person writing the letter would like to give them a call in the next couple of weeks to get their feedback. With relatively little subsequent cultivation, many of these families became Multiple-Year Donors.

Remember, these videos were only sent to people who had expressed a sincere interest in wanting to come to the event and were unable to make it at the last minute. The downside of this approach is that the seven-minute video, which was used as one element of the event program in between other live presenters, must now stand alone in the potential donor's home VCR. That is why the one-on-one follow-up is so important.

PRODUCTION TIME

Many groups use the lengthy lead-time needed to produce a video as an excuse for never making one. While more advance time for planning is best, most of the final shooting and editing can be done over a period of just a few days. We have worked with some groups that produce their entire video, start to finish, in less than two weeks' time and others that take up to six months to plan and produce their video.

Take the time to think through the video strategy that fits for your organization. It will be part of the lasting legacy you will be leaving.

CHAPTER 23

THE ONLINE POINT OF ENTRY

Once you have taken the time to refine and synthesize your Point of Entry content—namely the message you want to convey using the key Facts, frequently asked questions, Emotional Hook and Essential Story—you will know you have something you can take anywhere—even online.

While it may seem like a good idea, including your online Point of Entry as part of your organization's Web site may be more work than it is worth if you have not thought through your broader online strategy.

Odds are, unless you are the American Red Cross or a handful of other well-known charitable organizations whose work impacts the lives of millions of people in an urgent way everyday, people will not wake up in the morning and just happen to stop by your Web site to give you money. Furthermore, if they do visit your site, your terrific online Point of Entry may educate and inspire them, but what is the action you want them to take next? Exactly what is your step-by-step Web strategy?

The smart answer would be: to have them willingly give you their contact information, or, in the Raising More Money vernacular, to Capture their Name with permission. If your Web site did nothing more than that, after truly inspiring people online about your work, you would have accomplished a major feat—a true online Point of Entry!

The wrong answer would be to get them so excited that they

want to hurry to your "donate now" button and make a one-time gift—unless of course they give you their contact information willingly in the process of making the gift, and you have a system in place for following up with every single online donor.

In other words, the main purpose of an online Point of Entry is the same as of an in-person Point of Entry: to connect people directly to your work and to get them engaged enough that they will look forward to hearing from you in a one-on-one follow-up contact.

Having said that, let's look at how your online Point of Entry might work.

If you spend any time visiting nonprofit Web sites, you will quickly notice which ones grab you. Those boring dry sites will not do the trick. Nor will the ones with all the fancy streaming video of the disaster victims and hungry children, unless, in addition to moving you to tears, they also give you the facts. A great Web site that includes the three essential elements—Facts 101, Emotional Hook. and a legitimate way to Capture the Names of your guests—becomes a Point of Entry.

Some of the best online Points of Entry I have seen use stories and testimonials, combined with still or moving photos and music. Have your online Point of Entry be a virtual walk-through or tour of your organization.

You can easily include the same three handouts used at a live Point of Entry: the Fact Sheet, the Wish List and your standard brochure. These can be linked to your front page or introduced at the right time in the click-through virtual tour.

Your online Point of Entry must leave people in the same place your live Point of Entry left them, having answered the questions: How does the work of this organization change lives? How does it affect the life of one person or one family?

Do not trust your own instincts to gauge the impact of your online Point of Entry. Test it out on a few people to see if it is strong enough to educate and inspire them. Odds are it will need more emotion. The easiest way to add emotion is with stories. Those same compelling testimonials that have been so effective at your live Points of Entry can be put online in simple text format or embellished with photos and other graphics.

One advantage of the online format is that you can offer more than one story or program example. People can choose which stream or path they want to take through your Point of Entry. If for example your mission has three main components, your Web site can allow the visitor to click through to the Point of Entry that focuses on their area of interest. It might start with an overview of all three areas and then allow visitors to choose which facts and testimonial stories they would like to hear. Likewise, international relief organizations might have several examples of their work worldwide, allowing me to click on their programs in whatever part of the world I am most interested in learning about.

Make it easy on your visitors to stay engaged and to make it through your Point of Entry quickly. How many screens do they have to click through to get to the good stuff? Make the Point of Entry readily available once they arrive at your site.

If you adopt the approach that the main purpose of the online Point of Entry is to Capture the Name and contact information (or at least the e-mail address) of the visitor, with their permission, how are you going to do that?

Generally, you must "earn" that permission by offering people something in return. It should be something they would find useful, such as your newsletter, online briefings about issues related to your work, links to updates on your Web site that they will be interested in receiving. Otherwise, why would they voluntarily give you their contact information, especially when using a medium like the Internet that allows them to remain anonymous?

Conversely, your offer could be a request for information from them. This could include having a box or page for them to type in their comments about your Web site. It could be the opportunity to participate in a survey or join a chat room where they can have a forum to share their views. In exchange for offering any of these, you certainly have enough permission to ask for their contact information: name, address, phone number and, of course, e-mail address.

Unless you are prepared to conduct a full online donor relationship program, using all four steps of the model online, your objective should be to convert these online visitors to live visitors or guests at one of your organization's other events as soon as possible. The easiest way to do that is to follow up their visit to your site with an e-mail message asking for their feedback. Similar to our Follow-Up Call after a live Point of Entry, the purpose of the e-mail follow-up is to engage donors in a dialog—a give and take—according to our five-step follow-up process.

CHAPTER 24

POINTS OF ENTRY AND
THE HOLIDAY SEASON

Now that you understand the essential role of Points of Entry and Points of Re-Entry in the Raising More Money Model for building lifelong donors, let's look at the special components for using the model strategically during the holiday season.

WHAT MAKES THE HOLIDAY SEASON UNIQUE?

The value of the holiday season is that it is a time when people naturally connect with one another. We all get more invitations to attend social functions—whether for business, personal or charitable events. More people are talking to each other. Whether in person beside the punchbowl at a holiday party or by mail, fax or e-mail, this is a season of natural communication. This is a ripe opportunity for people to be talking about their association with your organization.

Second, the holiday season is the one time of year when we are legitimately encouraged to be kind, generous and caring towards others. People expect others to be doing good deeds during the holidays. We take pleasure in helping others at this time of year. Faith groups, employee groups, and families are all looking for projects to take on that demonstrate their compassion for others. People give time and in-kind goods: food baskets, toys, time to listen to others. It's a natural season for people to express their goodwill.

Third, this is a season of giving money. Punctuated by the end of the tax year, people naturally are taking stock of how they have fared financially, and many choose to make financial contributions now. The first organizations they will give to will be those they have remained most loyal to over the years—their "default charities." These are the organizations they feel connected to emotionally. There is no question about giving to these places. Next are the organizations they may have become involved with more recently. In those final weeks and months of the year, which "new" organizations will they give to? What will those fortunate organizations have done throughout the year to position their envelope in the "yes" stack of mail? Again, knowing that the majority of giving is done at year-end should be helpful information for your organization.

WHERE WILL YOU FOCUS?

The great temptation for most nonprofit organizations at the end of the year is to focus solely on asking for and receiving money. Think of the time and energy spent on this within your own organization: mailings, phone-a-thons, one-on-one Asks. If the cultivation work has been done throughout the year, this is a season of much asking and much giving. Your organization definitely needs to focus on picking the fruit.

However, in the frenzy of sending out holiday solicitation mailings and other year-end activities, the rich opportunities for connecting with people during this season are often overlooked. If you can broaden your organization's reach over the holidays to include those people who may be meeting you for the first time or reconnecting after a lapse of time, you will see many opportunities for deepening the connection and building lifelong donors.

What if you could use each occasion during the holidays strategically as a full-scale or mini-Point of Entry or Point of Re-Entry? Rather than having to go to the work of attracting people to your mid-year Points of Entry, what if you could take advantage of the already-established ways and places that people gather to tell or update them about the work of your organization?

Further, imagine that your cadre of volunteers and board members were all well-trained and deputized to be walking One-on-One Points of Entry wherever they go throughout the holiday season. Imagine the seeds that would be planted, or fruit that would be further ripened, ready for picking in the next year.

Your goal with your holiday Points of Entry is to make an indelible impression about the essential work of your organization. If this is their first contact, each visitor or guest should leave inspired and stirred up about your outstanding programs. If this is not their first contact, they should have been powerfully reconnected to your mission and acknowledged for their support. In any case, they should be looking forward to talking with you further in the New Year. They should be launched and on their way to becoming a lifelong donor.

HOLIDAY POINTS OF ENTRY: THE MESSAGE

Whether you will be planning One-on-One or group Points of Entry or Re-Entry, or converting existing holiday events to Points of Entry Conversion Events, there are two things to keep in mind at the holiday season. First, your guests will be busier than ever. Second, they want to be inspired and to make a difference.

Conveying your message in a clear, concise, inspiring way that will stand out amongst all the other holiday messages takes some careful planning. The place to start is with your well-honed Point of Entry in a Box format that has been tested over time. Then you can tweak it a bit for the holidays.

Making Your Needs Clear

More than ever, during the holidays, you must make the needs of your organization clear. This does not mean you will be asking for anything specifically at a Point of Entry, but rather that you are making it clear to people that their involvement with your organization is needed and would make a huge difference in their lives and in the lives of the people you serve.

Are you certain that your well-thought-out and choreographed Point of Entry is not giving people the message that you have everything handled—that you don't really need their help? If all they see is the pretty picture and the happy ending to the story, they won't know what's missing. They won't know where they fit in, where they can contribute. Conversely, if all they see is the sad story, they won't know the long-term positive difference that their support and involvement can make.

Make sure your Visionary Leader conveys a clear sense of a large gap between where you are now and where you are going. Use examples to make your points. For example: "Our mission is to provide these essential services to every child in foster care. Right now, there are three thousand five hundred children in temporary foster homes awaiting permanent placement with families. That is a lot of children still unserved." Or: "Now that you understand more about the advocacy services we offer, you can see why it is so important that we fulfill our mission to provide these services statewide (or nationally). We currently operate in only seventeen counties (or states). Our goal is to have a network of volunteers and an office in every county (or state). That takes time and resources."

Be sure your staff, board and volunteers are able to articulate your organization's needs as well. Arm them with specifics like your Fact Sheet and Wish List and have them practice talking about your programs and needs in their own words. "We need thirty more books in each classroom, forty more tutors, six more concerts per year, three more training programs per year, two hundred more computers, seventy-five more advocates."

Think this through as you prepare the various program examples you will be presenting at your events. Without actually asking people to give you specific things, are your needs clear? Is there enough urgency in the needs presented that people will feel compelled to take some type of action after the Point of Entry? At a minimum, you want people to be looking forward to your Follow-Up Call.

SPRUCING UP YOUR POINT OF ENTRY MATERIALS

Before we consider the many permutations of holiday Points of Entry and Re-Entry, let's be sure your basic Point of Entry materials are ready for the season. Just as you add candles or special photographs and flowers to your room decor at holiday time, it is a good idea to warm up your printed Point of Entry materials as well.

Fact Sheet

While the points to be made remain the same, you can certainly spin them a bit for the holidays. You may want to include seasonal trends, such as the number of elderly people in nursing homes with no family who visit them during the holidays, or the number of concert tickets your orchestra donates to school children and families over the holidays.

You may want to make new pie charts that highlight or summarize the percentage of your annual goals that have been achieved or remain to be reached. Do not underestimate the power of the Fact Sheet. Emotion alone won't build your organization loyal life-long donors. They have got to understand and be hooked by the facts as well.

Wish List

Be sure your Wish List is ready for the holidays. Remove any items you have already received and update the list with new items. Ask each program or department to list their top five needs. Have them be as specific as possible: large and small items, pots and pans, diapers, computers, gas for the van, a new music instructor or counselor.

Then compile them all into a single Wish List. You might consider listing them by area or department: "The nursery is wishing for _____, the maintenance staff is wishing for _____." It will let people know that you really need these items.

Print them up on holiday-type paper. Make enough copies so that you can distribute them generously throughout the season. Have them at your front door. Insert them in your newsletter. Have a little basket of them at your holiday parties and other events.

YOUR HOLIDAY POINT OF ENTRY OPPORTUNITIES

Look at your organization's calendar of events and activities that could become holiday Point of Entry Events. Include, for example, open houses, recognition events, volunteer group projects. Do not overlook the many program-related events like student music concerts or unscheduled alumni visits that tend to crop up over the holidays.

What if every event you produced this holiday season, from bake sales to black-tie galas, were treated like a Point of Entry or a Point of Re-Entry? Use the opportunity of having all these folks gathered together to educate and inspire them about your programs and services.

Furthermore, what if you treated every one-on-one 'social' conversation as a Point of Entry, and suggested that your staff and volunteers do the same? Imagine the ripple effects.

Think about how you could convert each holiday event or occasion into one of the following:

- Point of Entry in a Box
- One-on-One Point of Entry
- Point of Entry Conversion Event
- Point of Re-Entry (or Free Feel-Good Cultivation Event)

POINT OF ENTRY IN A BOX

You will definitely want to keep your regularly scheduled year-round Point of Entry Events going during the holiday season; just be sure to plan the dates of your holiday season Points of Entry strategically. Plot out on a calendar when your other holiday events and mailings are happening. When do the bulk of your pre-holiday inquiry calls come in? Is there a rush of calls in conjunction with your holiday open-house or some other event? Time your Points of Entry accordingly. I recommend planning one Point of Entry in a Box for the month of November, one in early December and one for January. That way, as people are calling in to inquire about other events or projects, your staff or volunteers can be inviting them to Points of Entry.

Most groups find they have more guests at these year-end Points of Entry. Whereas during the majority of the year, your volunteers and staff will be reaching out to people and inviting them to come and learn more about your organization, the holiday season should naturally generate a larger list of guests—people who are calling you to inquire about volunteer projects, articles they read about your needs, in-kind gifts. Your well-trained staff and volunteers who answer the phones can forward these inquiries to the development department. From there, you can sort out where they can best be accommodated and invite them to a Point of Entry Event.

Many organizations use the Point of Entry in a Box as a starting point to sort and refer the many groups that may approach them with projects over the holidays. By providing a compelling Point of Entry, each guest becomes more knowledgeable about your work, whether or not they choose to become more involved. For example, an employee work group had assigned one man the job of checking out several holiday project volunteer opportunities. The group selected a project, but the man was so inspired by the Point of Entry of another organization that he became personally involved with that organization and brought in a different group he was a part of.

THE ONE-ON-ONE POINT OF ENTRY

The holiday season presents innumerable opportunities for One-on-One Points of Entry, if you and your team are tuned into them—whether at formal holiday events sponsored by your organization or when your board, volunteers and other supporters are attending their own social events throughout the holiday season. The key, of course, is being aware of these mini-opportunities and being prepared to take advantage of them.

Recalling the format for the One-on-One Point of Entry discussed in Chapter 10, be sure that your team has practiced their "script" and can cover all of the points in the context of a brief, natural conversation.

1. Who we are—the name of your organization

2. Our top three programs

3. Three little known facts about our work

4. Why I work here

5. I'll never forget the story about …

6. Would you be interested in more information?

Your goal in these brief conversations is to cover enough material so that the person ends up saying, naturally, as you part: "Let's get together to talk more about that after the holidays."

POINT OF ENTRY CONVERSION EVENTS

How could you easily convert the many holiday community-group presentations you already have scheduled into Points of Entry? What about all of the corporate employee groups who call in wanting to take on a project for you over the holidays—taking a holiday dinner to a shut-in elderly person or having a class of school kids to serve dinner at your homeless shelter? How could you convert these opportunities to Points of Entry?

What if your organization does not have direct service opportunities for volunteers? How can you create volunteer opportunities that will be attractive to groups at this time of year? This approach is not just limited to human services organizations serving needy children and families. Arts, environmental, and advocacy groups, even membership organizations need ready projects or Units of Service that community groups can take on. What bite-sized chunk of your programs or services could they adopt or sponsor? Cleaning up a roadway, park or trail, helping with a year-end letter writing campaign to legislators, even helping to paint or clean an office can be satisfying, self-contained volunteer projects for eager groups at year-end. Your organization needs to be ready to publicize such opportunities in the summer and fall when faith-based and employee groups are selecting their year-end community service projects.

Then your challenge is to convert these project-centered volunteer experiences into bona fide Points of Entry. They must include the three essential ingredients of a Point of Entry: the Facts, the Emotional Hook and Capturing the Names with permission. This requires a time when everyone is seated for a brief presentation. A group of corporate employees coming to your office or center to do a one-time community service project is not expecting a long, drawn-out program. They are ready to get to work. Therefore you must make it brief.

Capturing Names with Permission

This is usually quite simple at a Point of Entry Conversion Event like a volunteer workday. Just have a sign-in table with a card for each person to complete with their name, address, phone number and e-mail. You can have a box on the sign-in card for people to check off if they would like to receive more information about your organization. People will expect to have to sign in as part of standard volunteer procedure within your organization. Furthermore, depending on the type of work they will be doing, you may have legal waivers of liability for them to sign. Handle all that at the beginning, then ask them to take a seat for a brief orientation about the day's project.

Facts and Emotional Hook

Use the next ten minutes to insert your official Point of Entry content. Have the appropriate person welcome the group. Next, a seven-minute talk from your Visionary Leader—or a shorter talk and video—followed by a three-minute live testimonial from a staff member, volunteer or consumer of your services. Make sure it is emotionally moving. Make sure each of the volunteers knows how much your organization values their time.

End with an overview of the project to be accomplished today, presented by your volunteer coordinator or the person in charge of the project. Let the volunteers know what a difference their work will make. Give specific examples of the numbers of people who will benefit from their work today. Keep stating the impact of what they will be doing today in terms of human lives. Remember, this is the holiday season. These "one-time" volunteers took on this project because they wanted to make a difference. This is your one and only opportunity to drive home the impact of your work and to make sure they remember your organization.

Because these volunteers will be doing hands-on work, they are likely to feel more connected when they leave. If possible, have your staff, volunteers, or even your clients be in attendance during the time of the project to keep the conversation focused on your mission. There are many opportunities to deepen the Facts and Emotional Hook during the "work project" part of the Point of Entry. In other words, even though the first ten minutes will seem like the only official program, if you plan properly, the entire volunteer work project can become an extended Point of Entry.

Follow-Up

Be sure to let people know at the end of the Point of Entry that you would appreciate their feedback after the event. Invite those who would like more information to come up and talk to you at the end of the presentation. Your first Follow-Up Call should be to the group organizer to gauge the overall response of the group. It is fine to include the others on your general mailing list and to call any others you or your team spoke with directly.

FREE FEEL-GOOD CULTIVATION EVENTS

Which events and activities that you already have scheduled over the holidays could become Free Feel-Good Cultivation Events? Consider the special recognition events for donors, board, volunteers or staff or student holiday performances, candlelight vigils, etc. Now that you are aware of the opportunity to insert a brief program element to update, inspire and re-connect prior supporters and friends with your current work, as well as educate their friends for the first time, how could you do that?

In fact, knowing that this event is scheduled to happen anyway, how could you expand its reach by inviting targeted sub-groups of donors or potential donors?

Remember, when done in accordance with the Raising More Money Model, these Free Feel-Good Cultivation Events also serve as Points of Re-Entry. Since the majority of the guests will be current or prior supporters, these events are an ideal opportunity to set the stage for everything you want to have happen next year. You have plenty of permission to share with them your accomplishments of the year that is ending as well as your dreams for next year and beyond. Now is the time to let them know if you are planning to launch a capital campaign, put together a matching gift challenge fund, or finally get that new program started. After all, as your "insider" group of supporters, it would be natural to share your plans with them early on in the process.

There is no asking for money done at these Free Feel-Good Cultivation Events, yet your Visionary Leader can easily plant the seeds with a "soft Ask," alluding to a letter or meeting after the first of the year that will detail the plans.

A WEALTH OF OPPORTUNITIES

As you begin to recognize the holiday season for the rich Point of Entry opportunities it provides, you will see more and more ways to insert the Facts and Emotional Hook into every holiday occasion, even those where you are unable to Capture Names. Here are some other examples:

- At the annual staff party, invite one or more satisfied families or clients to come back and speak about the difference the organization made in their lives. Be sure to acknowledge the families of the staff members for the support they have provided all year.

- Send a staff speaker with a copy of your video to make lunch presentations to all those community groups who want to "Adopt a Family" or "Adopt a Child" for the holidays. Make sure they know the year-round needs of that family or child and how they can keep contributing.

- At the annual volunteer or board recognition, give out awards that highlight the one-on-one impact of your work. If you are an arts organization, have a child or parent speak about what the theater or ballet has meant to your child. Use it as an opportunity to thank those who contributed the funds that enabled you to offer those free or discounted tickets. Showcase the volunteers who went out on the limb. Let them, or someone who benefited, tell how it changed their lives.

- At your bake sale or holiday fair, find a way to tell people what your organization does. Station an articulate, passionate staff member with a video at a booth near the front door. Or have the focus of the fair be on the accomplishments of your entrepreneurial, artistic or hi-tech urban kids.

THE BOTTOM LINE

The holiday season is high season for Points of Entry. It is the time of year when people are naturally connecting with each other, when they are open to caring and making a difference, when they want to hear those sentimental stories about how lives were changed. You don't have to stretch the truth or parade any "poster children." Just tell them the facts and share a firsthand story or testimonial.

If you plan for the holiday season with the Raising More Money Model in mind, you will see innumerable opportunities for Points of Entry of all types.

CHAPTER 25

LARGER CAMPAIGNS

If you adopt the Raising More Money Model and stick to it over time, you will eventually have enough Multiple-Year Donors that you might consider a larger campaign. These Free Feel-Good/ Point of Re-Entry Events become the logical way to launch a capital, endowment or major gifts campaign. That is because these events naturally honor and involve your loyal Multiple-Year Donors early on in the campaign, rather than relying on brand-new one-time donors.

LAUNCHING A CAPITAL CAMPAIGN

The following scenario describes how to use this model to launch a capital campaign that you plan to begin within about a year. Other (less than ideal) scenarios follow. This approach presumes that you have completed the entire Raising More Money cycle at least once, if not twice. That means you have conducted regular Point of Entry Events, done methodical follow-up and cultivation, and held at least one Ask Event or one cycle of one-on-one Asks. This gives you a base of loyal Multiple-Year Donors, with many at the $1,000 a year level. And you have regularly scheduled recognition and cultivation events to honor these donors—either formally or informally—and keep them informed of your progress.

Once you are certain you want to begin your pre-capital campaign strategy, your first step should be to host several Free Feel-

Good Cultivation Events for all donors of $1,000 or more. Either at your office, a board member's office, a private home or other meeting place, invite your loyal supporters to come to a Point of Re-Entry focused on the next phase of your dream—your capital needs.

As with any Point of Entry, you must give people the facts. This can be part of the Visionary Leader Talk. Why do you need the new building, new swimming pool, etc.? How many more people would it allow you to serve? Show them pictures or renderings of your new facility. Tell them how much money you will need to complete the campaign. Show them a gift table or pyramid chart with the number of gifts needed at each level, and name the opportunities you are thinking about using. You can still refer to these as tentative.

For the Emotional Hook, you could have a live testimonial from a staff member or volunteer about the immediate need your campaign seeks to raise money for. For example, they could tell what it feels like to turn people away due to lack of shelter space or medical examination rooms. If people have not recently seen the old facility, it is a good idea to walk them through it, if possible, highlighting the needs.

Next, the Visionary Leader or Board Chair makes a "soft Ask." "We wanted you, as the members of our Sponsor a Student Society, to be among the first to know about our plans. We'd like your thoughts and reactions. Does it make sense to you? Do you have any specific feedback about how to strengthen our plan? Think about it and we'll call you in the next few days to get your feedback."

Have your Visionary Leader or Campaign Manager make the Follow-Up Call. Follow the standard five-point format to solicit their feedback.

Then do whatever cultivation is necessary to have the donors be ready to give to capital. That means keeping in touch with people as you explore how to implement their suggestions. Stay in contact with them even if only to tell them why you are unable to follow through on their feedback. Many of these early supporters will become your best strategists and donors, and they will introduce others along the way.

When you begin to get the cues that people are ready to be asked, the Ask should be done one-on-one or with the couple, not in a group situation like our Ask Event. Each donor should be asked to give by someone they know personally who is deeply committed to the mission of the organization. If possible, the Visionary Leader or development staff person should be present. A good guideline is to ask the person to give only when you know they are ready to give. Then, when you ask, be sure one of the askers is someone you know the donor could not say no to.

Keep hosting your small Point of Re-Entry/Cultivation Events as the campaign is officially launched. Because you will be involving only loyal Multiple-Year Donors from the beginning, your campaign will have a solid base. This should enable you to complete your campaign in a shorter amount of time with fewer total donors.

Of course, if you want to open up the campaign to your larger community of donors, you are always free to do that.

MIDSTREAM IN A CAPITAL CAMPAIGN

The next scenario is less than ideal, although more common. In this scenario, your organization is already in the middle of a capital campaign or planning to launch a campaign in the next few months, knowing that you do not have a strong enough base of individual donors to complete the campaign. You are just beginning to launch your Raising More Money program for unrestricted funds.

You have wisely hired a consulting firm to do a capital campaign feasibility study. In their report to your board, they gave you a guarded recommendation that you could expect to raise—at the most—your minimum goal. The consulting firm put together a realistic plan for what it will take for you to reach the goal. It includes gifts from corporations, foundations and individuals. Now you have raised sixty to seventy percent of the money from corporations and foundations and are at a plateau as you begin the individual phase.

Most of the individuals on the potential donor list—other than your board members—are the obvious big-name donors in your community, yet they have no relationship to your organization. Perhaps you have realized, either midstream or early on in the campaign, that you may not have enough loyal individual donors to ensure a successful capital campaign. How, then, do you integrate the Raising More Money Model with an ongoing capital campaign?

I would recommend you do an internal "backfill" Point of Entry/Re-Entry program, where you fill in the gaps by focusing on reconnecting with your prior donors. Looking at each prior donor starting at the highest levels and working down the list, what does each of these donors need to be re-cultivated so that you are certain they are ready to give? Take the time needed for the fruit to ripen naturally. Lengthen your campaign timeline if necessary.

You want to avoid, at all costs, having even one donor be left with that uncomfortable feeling of being pressured to give too soon. This capital campaign may well be the first of many. Long after this first campaign is over, you want each donor to be a proud, lifelong friend and supporter of your organization. Though you might be tempted to rush the process by asking sooner and getting the gift, you don't want to alienate the donor in any way such that this might be their last gift.

Too often, organizations launch into a capital campaign ill-prepared and not heeding the warnings of the consulting firm. They think that somehow having such a firm means that the firm can magically produce donors the organization would not otherwise have.

Consulting firms do not bring you donors. Nor can they personally make Asks of donors. In the end, they will come to you for the names of donors and for the people who serve on the board or campaign committee who will make the Asks. There is no magic to it. Consulting firms earn their compensation. Their fees can be well worth paying, if you already have the donors and want to avoid hiring internal staff to manage an intensive campaign.

Too often, we see organizations ending their relationships with excellent consulting firms two-thirds of the way through a campaign because the organization did not heed the warnings to focus on deepening their base of solid donors early on. This situation is preventable. It is far better to lower your goal or elongate your campaign timeline in order to continue to cultivate and grow your base of life-long donors.

AT THE END OF A CAPITAL CAMPAIGN

If donors who have made a three-year capital campaign gift have been well taken care of and well listened to, they may be very willing to make a substantial multiple-year pledge for operating support.

Therefore, Free Feel-Good Cultivation Events, or Point of Re-Entry Events, can also be used near the end of a capital campaign to introduce the Multiple-Year Giving Society to a small group of strong supporters.

One strategy is to gather several capital campaign donors together and have one of the donors tell the others about your Multiple-Year Giving Society. In this case, the Facts and Emotional Hook need to be about the ongoing unrestricted operating needs of the organization to sustain or grow programs. Have one of your lead donors invite the others to step in at one of the upper giving levels or pool together their gifts to offer a challenge to other donors.

The intimacy of this small Free Feel-Good Cultivation Event is the ideal place to have this sort of conversation. Of course, these donors should be invited to your Ask Event as VIPs, whether or not they choose to give again.

FREE FEEL-GOOD EVENTS:
AN ESSENTIAL ELEMENT OF YOUR PLAN

Whether your goal is to fund operating needs, capital or endowment, these Points of Re-Entry or Free Feel-Good Cultivation Events are an essential—not optional—component of your overall fund development plan. They provide the structure that enables you to continually deepen your relationship with your most loyal of donors, as well as your volunteers.

MOVING AHEAD

CHAPTER 26

DESIGNING AND REFINING
THE IDEAL POINT OF ENTRY

B y now you probably have lots of ideas about how to design the ideal Point of Entry Event for your organization—as well as many unanswered questions.

This chapter will provide you with an outline of the key elements you will need before you can put together your first Point of Entry. This is your preliminary blueprint. It will need a great deal of testing and experimentation before you have refined all of the elements such that the sum of the parts is powerful and memorable. Do not expect this to happen naturally at your first Point of Entry Event.

Many groups spend months attempting to anticipate every detail of what they will need to put on the perfect Point of Entry, only to find out they have overlooked a key issue. For example, we worked with one organization that spent at least six months repainting and redecorating their main office, hiring artists to make beautiful display panels for their conference room, only to find, after experimenting, that the traffic and parking around this site were deterring visitors. They ended up moving the events to a more accessible satellite location, and attendance soared.

In other words, do not wait. The odds are, you will never be able to anticipate exactly how your Points of Entry will flow until you try actually conducting them. Do your best to fill out these worksheets with a core group of people from your team and then jump in and schedule your first event, even if you intentionally plan a small event for one or two guests. Once you have the first event, you will instantly become engaged in the process of experimentation and refinement that will lead to the ideal Point of Entry you will leave as a legacy.

Complete the worksheet at right: Designing Your Point of Entry in a Box. Then you will have thought through all the necessary elements for your first event, including the date it will take place!

Following is a Sample Point of Entry Agenda:

SAMPLE POINT OF ENTRY TIMELINE

8:00 Informal gathering time and sign-in, refreshments served, guests take their seats

8:05 Welcome and Introduction of Visionary Leader— Board member

8:10 Visionary Leader Talk—Executive Director, CEO or Founder

8:20 Questions and Answers—Development Director

8:25 Tour and/or testimonials—staff, volunteers, clients, program participants

9:00 End

Now, using the Sample Agenda, fill in the blanks for your own preliminary timeline:

YOUR PRELIMINARY POINT OF ENTRY TIMELINE

_____ **Informal gathering time and sign-in, refreshments served, guests take their seats**

_____ **Welcome and Introduction of Visionary Leader**

_____ **Visionary Leader Talk**

_____ **Questions and Answers**

_____ **Tour and/or testimonials**

_____ **End**

Designing Your Point of Entry in a Box

1. Name for your Point of Entry: _____
2. Frequency: _____
3. Time of Day/Week: _____
4. Venue (repeatable): _____
5. Format _____
   a. Greeter (title) _____
   b. Sign-In Person (title) _____
   c. Visionary Leader (title) _____
   d. Top Three Facts:
      1. _____
      2. _____
      3. _____
   e. Top Three FAQs:
      1. _____
      2. _____
      3. _____
   f. Emotional Hook
      1. Essential Story: _____
      2. How the Essential Story and others will be told
         ❑ Video of: _____
         ❑ Photos of: _____
         ❑ Tour of: _____
         ❑ Live Testimonial of: _____
         ❑ Letter/Audio Tape of: _____
   g. Handouts prepared by (date): _____
      ❑ Fact Sheet   ❑ Wish List   ❑ Brochure
   h. Thank-you and wrap-up person (title): _____
6. Who will follow up (title)? _____
   (They must attend Point of Entry)
7. When will your first Point of Entry take place? _____

CHAPTER 27

TURNING YOUR POINTS OF ENTRY INTO A SYSTEM

Finally, if you are committed to leaving your organization with Points of Entry as part of your legacy, you will need to turn the whole process into a system. I once had a participant in one of our workshops say, "I see now that our organization will be doing Points of Entry for life. Please help me figure out how to turn this into a system that will continue long after I'm gone." We did that, and his organization has continued that system for several years now that he has moved on.

Likewise, the school in Seattle where the Raising More Money Model was developed still continues to offer Point of Entry Tours every other Thursday morning, even though I left nearly ten years ago. Everyone involved with the school knows that, all month long, when new people call in to inquire about the school—whether to volunteer or to learn more—they are invited to the next scheduled Point of Entry. In other words, there is a system that lives on long after you are gone.

How can you do that?

First, of course, you have to design, test and refine your Point of Entry until it becomes the generic Point of Entry in a Box that is guaranteed to educate people and move them to tears in one hour. Even if they choose to do nothing further with your organization, you want to give them an experience they will never forget. After all, you never know who they will tell. You never know who they know. You never know what will change in their lives down the road. If you treated them well—and let them off the hook in the Follow-Up Call if they told you they really weren't interested in getting more involved —they will always think well of your organization and they will refer others.

SELECTING YOUR TEAM

Next, you need to shift the ownership of the system away from you. If the Point of Entry becomes know as "Bob's thing," it will never live on. The easiest way to do that—which you will need to do anyway to have the Raising More Money Model live on in your organization—is to put together your team. This is a group of five to seven people who agree to work on the implementation of the model for at least the next year.

I do not recommend that you necessarily convert your existing development committee into your team. Instead, put together a list of people you think would like to be involved in the process. Generally this will be your short list of people who are passionate about your work and have some time they can devote to working on this. Choose people you enjoy working with. A combination of staff, board and volunteers, including donors, works best. Perhaps there is a program person on your staff who is always inquiring about how the fundraising is going. Or perhaps they give you names of people in the community they think you should contact to learn more. Put these staff members on your team. The more breadth and diversity of roles and contacts your team members have, the better.

You can screen them for the job of team member by inviting them first to a Point of Entry, even if they haven't yet attended. For them, this will be a sample Point of Entry where they see firsthand the power of this approach. Make this "demo" event exceptional. Your goal is to have each of your potential team members become re-inspired and reconnected to their passion for the organization. Have it be your very best shot at what your ideal Point of Entry Events will look like in the future. In your one-on-one Follow-Up

Calls, ask each person for their candid feedback and make the changes they suggest wherever possible.

During your Follow-Up Call, tell them what you are trying to accomplish and ask if they would be interested in serving on the implementation team for the next year. Let them know the expectations of team members: that they help in designing and implementing the entire Raising More Money Model within your organization.

If they say yes, invite them to a one-day meeting or retreat where you will explain the whole process and design your Point of Entry system for the next year.

SUGGESTED AGENDA FOR THE FIRST TEAM MEETING OR RETREAT (4 HOURS TOTAL)

I.   Welcome and Introductions: 15 Minutes

Ask each person on the team to say why they are involved with the organization. What is their real connection to your work? This is a quick "passion retread" exercise, giving everyone on the team one minute to go around and tell their story. It will instantly energize the group and get you off to a powerful start.

Tell them what you intend to accomplish today: To put together a plan and a schedule for implementing the Raising More Money Model over the next year.

II.   Put the Point of Entry in Context of the Larger Raising More Money Model: 60 Minutes

"You have all attended one of our Point of Entry Events over the last month. Perhaps you didn't know that that event is the first step in a larger system for building our base of lifelong individual donors. It is a model—a system—that we would like to adopt for our organization. Let me explain the other steps in the system quickly to you."

Then walk them through a demonstration of the model. The easiest way to do this is to show them the Raising More Money (47 minute) video that gives an overview of the entire model. It clearly demonstrates how the Point of Entry system will lead to more mission-based lifelong donors for your organization. They will like this. Allow time for discussion afterwards.

III. Treasure Maps: 60 Minutes

Next, begin the process of brainstorming as a team who to invite to your Point of Entry Events. Given the person-to-person nature of this model, it only makes sense to start with the people who already are connected to you in some way. You can branch out from there, following the stream of passion and natural word-of-mouth connections that link people. Before you know it, the whole system will snowball.

The quickest and easiest way chart this all out is to make a Treasure Map for your organization with your team (see Chapter 7). Let the Treasure Map become messy and overwhelming. It will help your team members to see the rich treasure at your disposal. All those resources that these groups have in abundance are your resources! After all, these people and groups are on your organization's Treasure Map.

Next, give each person on the team a piece of paper and ask them to make a personal Treasure Map. Go through the same steps: Have them put themselves in the middle and surround themselves with all the groups they come into contact with on a regular basis: their work associates, their friends, their family, the other parents at their kids' schools, friends from their other hobby groups or interests—the gym, the book club, the church group. Have them go back and make a list of at least ten people they could easily invite to a Point of Entry, now that they understand what it is and trust the process.

If there are people on their Treasure Maps they would not feel comfortable inviting yet, you might suggest they use the Treasure Map Interview questions to engage these people in a dialog about your organization's work.

IV. Plan Out the Year: 45 Minutes

Look ahead for a full year. Identify any other objectives you wish to accomplish with your Point of Entry program. How many total guests do you want to have? If you are planning to put on the Free One-Hour Ask Event, how many Table Captains will you need to have the number of guests you desire? Perhaps you will discover that you need to have more frequent Points of Entry than once a month.

List out all of the events that you normally put on in a year. Could any of them become Point of Entry Conversion or Free Feel-Good Cultivation Events? If so, what is your timeline for converting them? (See also the Conversion Chart in Chapter 12.)

Consider who else you need to "bless" your plan, officially or unofficially, so that it will be successful. Figure out your strategy for getting their support.

V. Plan Your Point of Entry Program: 30 Minutes

Set a goal for the number of people you want to attend your point of Entry Events over the next year.

Next, get out the calendar and create a schedule for your Points of Entry in a Box. How often are they going to happen and when? Plot it all out on a calendar. You can vary the days of the week or time of day until you have zeroed in on your ideal timing. These Points of Entry in a Box will become the mainstay of your system, so you need to schedule them first. I recommend at least one a month.

Publish the dates of your Point of Entry Events for the next year in your internal calendars and bulletin boards. Give copies to the board and staff.

Print up business cards with the name and address of your organization on the front and the dates of the upcoming Point of Entry Events and driving directions on the back. Have stacks of these cards available in your office reception area, at board and volunteer meetings for people to carry with them throughout the month.

Where are all those guests going to come from? Perhaps you can start by asking each team member to host one event and invite the people on their personal Treasure Maps.

Deputize additional ambassadors to help you reach other groups on your Treasure Map. Schedule additional Point of Entry Events for your board and other special committees, including, for example, subgroups of volunteers, donors, vendors, and other professionals in the community. Assign the most appropriate person on the team to be the liaison to each special group. Your board and committee members will need support in actually having their friends and colleagues attend your Points of Entry. Do not assume that their sincere interest in inviting people will translate into real guests attending your monthly event. What kind of follow-up support might they need?

Invite board members and team members to become guest hosts at each Point of Entry Event, to welcome the visitors on behalf of the board. While you are certainly not expecting these hosts to fill the room with their friends or colleagues, it will be a convenient time for them to bring along that special person or two who they have been meaning to invite.

VI. Team Structure: 30 Minutes

You will need one person to coordinate the team; ideally, that will be the director of development.

Depending on the rate at which you will grow your program and the number of Points of Entry, Cultivation Events and Ask Events, you may be able to get the job done with as few as three active team members. Ideally, you will have five to seven working members in addition to the cadre of volunteers who are already on board to help produce some of the larger events.

Let other team members choose which area they would like to be responsible for. For example, you may want one person to be in charge of Point of Entry RSVPs or scheduling future "on the road" Points of Entry. Each of the other events will need coordination as well.

While the process may seem a bit complicated, putting on Points of Entry is relatively easy, once you get all the pieces in place. It will come as no surprise that the most labor-intensive part is the follow-up. Again, if you have paid fund development staff, I recommend they be in charge of follow-up, to ensure consistency, timeliness and accuracy in tracking feedback. That way, too, the historical record of all contacts can be stored in the organization's database.

Finally, schedule your team meetings for the next year at the rate of one or two per month and agree on a procedure for reporting results to the team leader between scheduled meetings.

CHAPTER 28

MOVING AHEAD

Congratulations! You are ready to go—or nearly so. You see, just like the lifelong relationships your organization seeks to develop over time with your donors, the Point of Entry is a work in progress. It will require constant testing and experimentation, feedback and refinement.

Remember that this book is designed to be a reference book. Keep it handy. Refer to it as you refine each aspect of your program. As you get started, you will likely find yourself focusing on one or two aspects of the Point of Entry Event—perhaps the venue or Fact Sheet or your Essential Story, for example. Once those components become tried and true, you may find yourself becoming curious about other ways to convey the Emotional Hook or how to take your Point of Entry on the road to a group of corporate employees or a faith-based group's monthly meeting. That is when you may want to pick up this handbook again to refresh yourself on how to convert those events to Points of Entry.

While at first glance, the Point of Entry seems rather obvious and simplistic, you may be surprised to find yourself becoming more and more intrigued with its more subtle aspects. For example, the timing and sequencing of the program elements may need to be adjusted once you have tested out several options. You may notice yourself becoming more observant of the guests' reactions to words or phrases, graphics or music.

The most important thing to keep in mind in designing the consummate Point of Entry is that you are going through the critical, albeit sometimes excruciating, process of synthesizing your organization's multi-faceted work into one succinct, educational and inspiring hour. To do that well—to design, test and refine a quality Point of Entry that predictably delivers a consistent impact once a week or once a month for the next ten years—will be leaving a powerful legacy for your organization. It will be a legacy that honors the true mission of your work and lays a solid foundation for your relationships with lifelong donors.

BIBLIOGRAPHY

Godin, Seth. *Permission Marketing.* Simon & Schuster, 1999.

Independent Sector, *Giving and Volunteering in the United States.* 2001.

Jensen, Rolf. *The Dream Society: How the Coming Shift from Information to Imagination Will Transform Your Business.* McGraw Hill, 1999.

Kaplan, Ann E., Editor. *Giving USA 2001: The Annual Report on Philanthropy.* American Association of Fundraising Counsel (AAFRC) Trust for Philanthropy, 2001.

Newtithing Group. *National Affordable Donations In 2001.* 2001.

Nichols, Judith E., Ph.D, CFRE. *Changing Demographics: Fund Raising in the 1990s.* Bonus Books, 1990.

Rosenberg, Claude, Jr. *Wealthy and Wise—How You and America Can Get the Most Out of Your Giving.* Little, Brown and Company, 1994.

ABOUT THE AUTHOR

Terry Axelrod, the founder of Raising More Money, trains and coaches nonprofit organizations nationally and internationally in how to build self-sustaining individual giving programs.

As an accomplished fundraiser, founder of three charitable organizations and professional social worker, Terry is committed to abundant funding for the vital work of the nonprofit sector. She has been raising funds for organizations for the past twenty-five years. Like many fund development professionals, she began with no formal training or experience, out of the need to raise funds for a home health care program, which she co-founded in the mid-1970s. Beginning with a seemingly unrelated special event, the running of the modern-day Greek Marathon, she learned by trial and error what it takes to convert on-time "special event" donors into true, lifelong donors.

Subsequently she served as the first Director of Development at the Graduate School of Social Work at the University of Washington. Then, for twelve years, she worked in the private sector as a securities broker-dealer for a national investment firm, while founding two other nonprofit housing organizations.

From 1992 to 1995, Terry worked with Zion Preparatory Academy, an exceptional inner-city school in Seattle, Washington, that had never before done any formal fundraising. Focusing intently on individual giving, the school raised more than $7 million for unrestricted operating support and a capital campaign, and was nationally recognized in a cover story for the *Chronicle of Philanthropy*.

Realizing that this small, relatively unknown school had been a beneficiary of individual funding of unprecedented magnitude, Terry set about to distinguish the principles that had made all that fundraising seem relatively effortless. The result is the Raising More Money Model, which is now taught to teams from organizations of all types and sizes in an intensive two-day workshop with subsequent coaching sessions to ensure its successful implementation.

ADDITIONAL INFORMATION
AND RESOURCES

Visit our Web site at www.raisingmoremoney.com to:

- Subscribe to our free bi-weekly electronic newsletter, the Raising More Money E-New$;

- Register for one of our many free or inexpensive introductory sessions;

- Register for the two-day Raising More Money 101 Workshop;

- Browse the Raising More Money archives for additional information on building a self-sustaining individual giving program.

To order additional books or videos
about Raising More Money,
please call 1-888-322-9357, or visit
www.raisingmoremoney.com/publications

INDEX